"A compelling, tragic  Indian slum community. count of her joy, fear, faith eying alongside some of th our planet today. In the p ..ove herself, her neighbors and her God with greater authenticity."

—Scott Bessenecker, author of *The New Friars* and *Overturning Tables*

"Beautifully written, the reader is drawn into the inner lives and outer world of Trudy and her husband Andy as they seek to serve Christ in an Indian slum. This is a story of faithfulness in the face of seeming failure. No young idealistic Westerner who is planning overseas service can do without this book."

—Charles Ringma, theologian, activist, and author of *In the Footsteps of an Ancient Faith*

"Filled with beautiful, messy stories and honest reflections about faith, *God in Disguise* is a journey toward the deep, unexplainable hope that comes only through real-life experiences that go beyond scriptural platitudes or blind certainty. Trudy's story will bring hope and connection to those longing to find God in the most unlikely places."

—Kathy Escobar, Co-Pastor of The Refuge and author of *Faith Shift: Finding Your Way Forward When Everything you Believe is Coming Apart*

"Few people have travelled so far, geographically, and spiritually, as Trudy. Her compelling story is about the quest to rediscover the true teachings of Jesus, a journey that takes us from suburban America to the slums of India. In the process, we are deeply challenged and inspired to live a different way. A story beautifully told."

—Craig Greenfield, author of *Subversive Jesus* and founder of Alongsiders International

God in
Disguise

Losing and finding Jesus at the ends of the earth
and the limits of my soul

TRUDY TAYLOR SMITH

God in Disguise
Losing and Finding Jesus at the ends of the earth and the limits of my soul

Scripture quotations taken from the HOLY BIBLE, NEW IN-TERNATIONAL VERSION®. NIV®. Copyright © 1973, 1978, 1984 by International Bible Society. Used by permission of Zondervan. All rights reserved worldwide.

ISBN-13: 978-1545511749

ISBN-10: 1545511748

Cover design by Andrea Armstrong

Cover photo by Trudy Taylor Smith

Printed in the United States of America

AUTHOR'S NOTE

In order to protect the privacy of my friends and neighbors in India, the names of people and places in this book have been changed. However, the people and the stories you will encounter in these pages are entirely real. By relying on my own journal entries and blog posts from that time in addition to memory, I have sought to present the most accurate account possible of my experiences.

While I lived in the slum, the majority of my life—and certainly all of my interactions with neighbors—happened in a mixture of Hindi and Urdu. For that reason, a few Hindi/Urdu words and phrases appear throughout this book as part of my endeavor to help readers enter into the world of my neighborhood. The plural forms of these words do not follow English conventions; for example, the plural form of *sari* is *sariya*, and the plural form of *mazar* is *mazare* or *mazarat*. But for the sake of being able to more smoothly massage these words into English sentences, I will stick to using the English grammatical structure of adding "s" to nouns to pluralize them, even though this is technically incorrect.

.

CONTENTS

IV. HEALING

PROLOGUE

If you quiet yourself to hear God's voice, you will likely begin to hear things that are comforting and alarming, loving and disturbing, wonderful and terrifying. That voice will call you beyond yourself and invite you to walk out to the edges of your certainty and safety and leap into unknown territory, where your heart will be split open by the things you will discover in your neighbor and in yourself. As you journey onward, your heart will burst with compassion. Yet if you venture even further, your scarred heart will be melded to the heart of God, and you will begin to mend. You will love yourself more than you ever imagined. You will discover that your neighbor—and your enemy—are yourself. And you will fall in love with this wild God who companions you on the journey, over and over again.

There are many reasons that might propel us to venture to the edges of our certainty and leap after this God of love. But the journey, ultimately, is not about guilt or responsibility, right or wrong, adventure, justice, or anything else. It is about love.

I.
CERTAINTY

1988-2012

"The opposite of faith is not doubt, it's certainty."

— Anne Lamott

1
FEAR AND PUNISHMENT

Texas, 1988-2006

I spent my first eighteen years in the same small Texas town, which was also my dad's hometown. We were members of the same church he had attended as a boy, and until I was twelve years old, we lived in my great-grandfather's house in an older neighborhood. My family lived comfortably in our mostly white, wealthy suburb, and nearly everyone we knew was both an evangelical Christian and a patriot. Aside from high school football games on Friday nights during the fall, the annual Fourth of July parade down Main Street and the concert and fireworks in the park afterward were the biggest community events of the year.

I was a serious child, and I spent a lot of time in my own imaginary world. In kindergarten, my mom realized several months into the school year that I didn't know the name of a single classmate, and so she gave me the assignment of telling her the name of one more child in my class every day until I had learned them all. In first grade, I once got into trouble for absentmindedly singing Beach Boys songs while standing in line. I had already been told to be quiet, but I was so preoccupied with the song playing in my mind that it was hard for me to tell when it had spilled out into the real world. I was often content to play by myself for hours, making up stories in my head. Sometimes I would climb twenty feet up into an oak with a pen and a notebook to write these stories down.

Along with my younger sister and brother, I was home-schooled for several years, largely because it was important to my parents to pass on their Christian values and their perspective of history—most importantly, their beliefs about the creation of the world and the creation of the United States. I was usually able to finish the day's assignments in a few hours, and then I had the rest of the day to play outside in our large backyard, jumping on our trampoline, playing in the three-story fort we built with our dad, or climbing the spreading branches of the massive, hundred-year-old southern live oak trees that shaded our yard.

We always had one or two dogs around—usually golden retrievers or labs, though we once had a beagle that frequently escaped and caused my parents a lot of grief by ending up in the dog catcher's custody and having to be bought back. For awhile, we also kept rabbits (until they multiplied beyond what we were able to accommodate). My parents originally bought three of them—one for each of my siblings and me—thinking they were all female. But within a few weeks, the first of several litters of baby bunnies proved that the rabbit hutch was not the chaste cloister we had imagined! There were also plenty of blue jays, mockingbirds, and cardinals in the backyard, and I would occasionally get the chance to "rescue" baby birds that fell out of their nests. When a baby blue jay with an injured leg was eaten by a cat before I could nurse it back to health, I cried as though a family member had died.

Throughout my childhood years, I was fascinated with other cultures and with Asia in particular. My natural curiosity about the world, supplemented with a steady diet of missionary biographies, prayer updates, and fundraising campaigns for missions at my church, led me to decide by the time I started kindergarten that I would move to the other side of the world when I grew up. Due to the shady oaks and to some sort of flooding incident with a previous tenant, there was no grass in our backyard. My parents were chagrined by the yard's refusal to cooperate with their vision of a thick, luxuriously green lawn—and my mother understandably hated the mud we kids tracked into the house every time it rained—but I took great joy in organizing my siblings around planting bean gardens and making mud bricks to bake in the sun so that we could build our own hut and pretend to live in a faraway village.

By the age of ten, I started learning two foreign languages on audio cassette. Mandarin Chinese was the language that really captured my imagination, but since we were living on the Gulf coast of Texas, my mom didn't expect I would get much use out of an Asian language, and she bribed me into learning Spanish by allowing me to listen to the Chinese lessons only after I had finished the lessons in Spanish.

At the beginning of my seventh-grade year, we moved from my great-grandfather's house into a new, bigger, custom-built house a few minutes' drive away. It came with a two-acre, grassy yard, a gate, and a bedroom for each of us—something my sister and I were thrilled about after sharing a room for years. My world was sheltered and small; the town where I lived was the kind of place where many people grew up hanging out with the same friends from first grade to high school graduation, went away to university somewhere else in the state, and eventually returned to raise their own children. But for some reason, as far back as I can remember, I always knew that I would leave.

Growing up in a Southern Baptist church, I encountered Christianity as a religion of answers. Peace came from knowing everything important—whether you would go to heaven or hell if you died that night in your sleep, what you needed to believe in order to be saved, and the difference between right and wrong. *The Bible is a how-to manual for life*, I heard from the pulpit, *just like the user's manual that comes with a new car*. Just as concrete, irrefutable, and easy to understand as that.

Church membership was based on intellectual assent to a set of beliefs. Being a Christian meant you agreed with everything on that list, and you obeyed everything God commanded. There was a lot of talk about God's grace, but it was always in the context of God choosing to forgive human beings even though we were incorrigibly evil sinners who, as depraved wretches, deserved eternal damnation. Grace meant that in spite of God's holy wrath burning against us, we were being rescued from the fate of endless torture because Jesus had taken on the gruesome punishment we deserved. And once we accepted this "free" gift, our proper response was to feel guilt, shame, and remorse for having put Jesus through that whole ordeal. During youth worship services, we stood in darkened rooms, tearfully making our way through emotional songs about the crucifixion as we were encouraged to reflect on how our sins had nailed Jesus to the cross.

Conversion, in the Baptist tradition, was a moment when you recognized that you were a sinner, asked God to forgive you, and were spiritually "born again." You prayed the sinner's prayer, you invited Jesus into your heart, and you walked down the aisle during the altar call and told the pastor you wanted to be baptized. It was important for you to know exactly when this conversion moment had happened. People at church would write down the day and the year in the front covers of their Bibles as their "spiritual birthday," and preachers would often begin their "invitations" at the end of a sermon by asking whether we were all certain of the exact time we had asked Jesus to come into our hearts. *Know that you know that you know*, they would say. As I heard every year during Vacation Bible School, the process was as simple as learning your ABC's: Admit (that you are a sinner), Believe (that Jesus died and rose again), Confess (that Jesus is Lord).

I first experienced this moment of conversion when I was five years old, but no matter how many times I went through the ABC's, I still felt sinful and uncertain that Jesus had really come into my heart. Had I said the right words? Did I really believe? Since I still hadn't gotten into a "quiet time" routine of reading the Bible every day, did my conversion really count? And what if I forgot something I should have confessed? Would God still forgive me for that unacknowledged sin, or would I find out after I died that He had been angry about it my whole life? Every time there was another altar call, I felt condemned by these doubts and fears, and I would pray again for Jesus to come into my heart. *Know that you know that you know.*

As I performed this regular maintenance on my salvation, I felt tortured by uncertainty, because I didn't know which one of those times was my real conversion. I worried that God might even be angry at me for doubting His presence in my life after He was already there. There was just no winning with God. *Know that you know that you know.*

I never questioned the rules or the outward forms of the faith I was taught. I was certain about what was true. I was certain about what the Bible said. I was certain about the right formulas. I memorized large swaths of Scripture, and I could recite the books of the Bible in canonical order from Genesis to Revelation—including a Texas-accented butchering of the ancient Hebrew names of all the minor prophets. What I questioned was my own goodness and lovability. What I questioned was my internal experience: I agonized over my inability to get it all right, and despite all our singing and praying about peace, I never felt very peaceful about this loving Father whom I was supposed to trust entirely, but from whose deadly wrath I needed protection.

So when I was eight years old, I secretly lost my religion and decided to give up on prayer for a few years. I was worn out by my constant fear of unconfessed sin and the endless, scrupulous confessions that kept me awake at night, trying to remember anything I might have thought or done wrong.

Memories of church during this time are etched into my mind with fear. I remember the covered elements casting a harsh silver glare up at me as I sat in the balcony before communion. The carpet of the church was blood-red, but the actual body and blood of Jesus only made an appearance four times a year, and I always dreaded their somber presence. Each time we took the Lord's Supper, it seemed the church was rehearsing for Judgment Day. The pastor would always read the same passage, one that struck fear into my heart: "So then, whoever eats the bread or drinks the cup of the Lord in an unworthy manner will be guilty of sinning against the body and blood of the Lord. Everyone ought to examine themselves before they eat of the bread and drink from the cup. For those who eat and drink without discerning the body of Christ eat and drink judgment on themselves. That is why many among you are weak and sick, and a number of you have fallen asleep."[1]

A numbness seeped into my legs and a cold sweat prickled the nape of my neck, because I was certain that I was about to eat and drink judgment upon myself. Surely it was a sin to eat at the Lord's table if you had given up on Him and hadn't talked to Him any time recently. Yet I had no choice but to drown myself in potential damnation by eating and drinking unworthily, because I was afraid of

---

[1]   1 Corinthians 11:27-30

the immediate punishment that I imagined might be in store for me if I refused to eat and drink at all—and then had to explain myself to my parents.

I was banking on being able to repent later, but of course the terrifying thought of dying during my premeditated season of godlessness sometimes kept me up at night, too. I viewed these prayerless years as a break, hoping that when I was a bit older I might get better at being holy, and my spiritual life would get easier. But because I believed wholeheartedly that I was doomed to hell apart from Jesus, walking away from God completely was never an option for me. Even as I privately withdrew from the spiritual life, I assumed that as an adult, I would ultimately devote myself to God and make good on my plans to become a missionary.

After reading the *Left Behind* book series a year or two later, missing the rapture joined my list of spiritual terrors. Every time I was unable to locate my other family members in the house, I assumed it had happened. My worst fear was Jesus coming back before I had a chance to sort things out with Him. There were other fears, too—of sharks, ghosts, being murdered, or accidentally murdering someone else in my sleep like I had seen depicted in a disturbing episode of a crime show called *Unsolved Mysteries*. I also suffered a severe phobia of the dark, which lasted into my early twenties.

Then, at the age of twelve, I decided to give the whole God thing another try. I considered myself fortunate to have survived four years of depravity, so when I felt God reaching out to me, I knew I'd better take advantage of the opportunity. I was sitting by myself on a rock underneath a cedar tree with a trunk that fanned apart as branches growing directly out of the ground, creating a sort of protected dome of a "room," where I could look out at the yard from beneath the low-slung eaves of its boughs. It's hard for me to describe the specific events of that divine encounter, because I have layered so many different versions of the story on top of one another in my countless retellings since that day. Each time, I have filtered the experience through whatever theological understanding I currently hold, and my understanding has continued to evolve over the years. I do remember, in my grave, precocious, twelve-year-old way, beginning to think deeply about my life and about how I was wasting it. Then I felt a sense of welcome from God—an offer: He was there to listen to me if I was ready to talk to Him, and I could start over with a clean slate that very day, if I wanted to. Looking back, I name that movement toward me as grace. But at the time, I felt fear in the presence of God. I sensed His closeness, and so my heart was pounding and tears came to my eyes: like the baby birds I sometimes found in my backyard, I trembled from fear even in the hands of a loving rescuer, simply because those hands seemed so big and so unpredictable to me.

Fear and longing remained tangled up together for me as I entered adolescence. Knowing without a shadow of a doubt that everyone who died without believing in Jesus would go to hell, I spent my teenage years wholeheartedly praying, worshipping, attending Bible studies, and witnessing to as many people as possible—not to mention participating enthusiastically in whatever dangerous or zany activities the youth ministry dreamed up. Even eating bananas through panty hose or sacrificing our bodies in life-threatening summer camp games like buck-buck seemed to take on a spiritual sheen when they were connected with church. While on short-term mission trips in junior high, I was a boney little ninety-pound evangelist who would approach drunken men more than twice my size in the street to present the plan of salvation and ask if there was any reason they couldn't accept Jesus as their Lord and Savior right then.

I loved God. I was terrified of God. It was hard to distinguish between the two.

Know that you know that you know.

Another thing I never questioned was God's gender. He was our Father. He was a King. He took an anatomically male form when He revealed Himself on earth. Every pastor I had ever seen was a man. God was unquestionably male, and His exclusively masculine persona was such a fixture in my universe that I hardly noticed it. *Know that you know that you know.*

But then in junior high, the idea began to chafe a little. I was at a small youth group gathering in someone's home, where the youth pastor (a man, of course) was delivering a lesson on a New Testament passage that forbade women to teach men. Perhaps it was 1 Timothy 2:11–12: "A woman should learn in quietness and full submission. I do not permit a woman to teach or to have authority over a man; she must be silent. For Adam was formed first, then Eve." I don't remember which passage we were studying, but what impressed itself on my consciousness at that moment—and what I carried with me from that moment forward—was a sense of frustration and disappointment.

At thirteen years old, I did not feel free to question God, much less to feel anger toward Him, but the shocking idea sunk in that I was somehow inferior to the boys sitting around me on the floor—even the ones who immaturely goofed off during Bible studies instead of contributing thoughtful answers and questions as I did. I felt suddenly embarrassed and ashamed of myself in front of them, as if I had just been dissed—by the youth pastor, by the apostle Paul, by God. I was utterly confused, and the youth pastor himself didn't pretend to understand the rather arbitrary teaching. He shrugged almost apologetically and said something to the effect of, "Sorry, ladies. I didn't write it, but that's what it says." I was raised in a religious atmosphere of, "The Bible says it, I believe it, that settles it." The Bible said it, and so I believed, but the matter was far from settled.

At youth camps throughout my junior high and high school years, girls could get in trouble at any time for wearing shorts that were too short or tops that were too low, but the double standard of modesty was most glaring at the pool. The boys we had crushes on were free to swim around shirtless without a second thought, but we girls were required to either wear a one-piece swimsuit to cover our top halves, or to wear a big, baggy T-shirt (a dark one, mind you) over a two-piece suit in order to "keep our brothers from stumbling"—poor, helpless things. We had this mysterious power over them—they were apparently powerless against the sight of female flesh, but woe to us if we became the door through which temptation entered. Our bodies were their spiritual kryptonite, and intentionally or accidentally exposing our male peers to them was a sin we were frequently reminded to avoid. Lust was presented as a regrettable but inevitable reality for boys, but arousing lust with immodest clothing was a sin that could come to define a girl. I knew to call these girls sluts (and to avoid becoming one) long before I realized that there was no equivalent epithet for a boy.

2
QUESTIONS AND CRACKS

California, Argentina, Thailand, and China, 2006–2011

When I graduated from high school, I decided to leave Texas and relocate to the West Coast to attend Pepperdine University, intent on surfing and taking in the excitement of Los Angeles. I saw this as the logical first step toward moving out of the country altogether. My family worried that after living in California, I would no longer fit comfortably into the culture that had raised me. Though their fears ended up being realized, the changes in me didn't come from the afternoons I spent strolling down Venice Beach, but during the semesters I spent studying abroad.

Growing up, I had been taught that my country could do no wrong. We were "the good guys," and even God was on our side—capitalism, patriotism, and discipleship all went hand in hand. But during a semester abroad in Argentina, I learned about the CIA's political machinations in Central and South America to overthrow democratically elected leaders, train soldiers in the art of torture, and use bloodshed to the advantage of America's national interests.

And during a semester abroad in Thailand, I encountered the underbelly of free trade when I met villagers who had witnessed the staff of a well-known multinational company impersonating medical professionals to tout the benefits of formula over breastfeeding. These campaigns resulted in infant deaths when impoverished mothers could not afford enough to feed their babies or mixed the formula with dirty water. The once-benign corporate labels that covered my food and my clothes now took on the weight of sweatshops and the exploitation of workers in the developing world. My comfort took on a hue of excessive wealth when placed next to the poverty I had seen. Even my citizenship took on a darker aspect, as I knew that my protection and prosperity were ensured by the suffering of others.

Around this time, a classmate loaned me *Come Be My Light*, a collection of private letters published after Mother Teresa's death, which detailed her difficult internal experience and the love for Jesus that had driven her to spend decades serving the poor. I had read Jesus' words in Matthew 25:40 many times: "Truly I tell you, whatever you did for one of the least of these brothers and sisters of mine, you did for me." Yet through Mother Teresa, I was first confronted with the reality of Jesus' continuing incarnation in the "distressing disguise" of poverty. Her lifetime commitment to serving Jesus in the poor through small acts of great love both thrilled and intimidated me. I longed for that kind of single-minded devotion to God, and I felt intense compassion for the suffering people she described in India. It didn't escape my notice, however, that the path the Calcutta saint had chosen was one that had been difficult and often painful.

During those semesters abroad, I also met Christian pacifists in the flesh for the first time. In Thailand, one of my classmates was a Mennonite student from Messiah College in Pennsylvania who was committed to social justice. This Mennonite was convinced that nonviolence was central to Jesus' message, and, practicing what he preached, he absorbed verbal "violence" and incredulity from me during many lengthy conversations in which my tone made it clear that I doubted his intelligence for holding such an "extreme" view. Despite my open hostility, he patiently explained his beliefs, answered my questions with thoughtful replies, and loaned me books by theologians who grounded their commitment to nonviolence in Scripture.

I had been reading theology since high school, but I had never before come across biblical scholars who interpreted Jesus' eventual torture and death at the hands of the Roman state in terms of enemy love and nonviolent resistance to evil. I began to study not only the life of Jesus, but also secular history, through a new lens, learning about the efficacy of nonviolent movements led by Gandhi, Martin Luther King, Jr., and others. As I continued to explore these new ideas, my skepticism was eventually replaced with the conviction that rejecting violence was an important part of following Jesus.

During this season of significant personal upheaval while studying in Thailand, I also became friends with Andy, who would later become my husband. Born to Canadian parents in the U.S., Andy grew up as a missionary kid in Latin America and Spain. Some of his earliest memories were of wandering through open-air markets with his mother in Ecuador and smuggling Bibles into Morocco under his jacket as a third-grader. He also remembers driving across America in his family's Chevy van on a support-raising tour of churches, visiting his grandparents in Toronto, and living for a short interval in a shabby "missionary house" in upstate New York. As the fourth of five children, and with his large family constantly ricocheting from one culture and continent to another, Andy learned from an early age to adapt to whatever new environment he found himself in. He was easy-going, accommodating, and could make friends with anyone. He had also inherited from his father a sense of adventure and an incurable wanderlust; his home was the world, and yet it was nowhere in particular.

My experiences overseas and then my return to the U.S., where I encountered poverty and systemic injustice in my own country, right there in downtown Los Angeles, changed my politics, my theology, my everything. During the maladjusted summer following my year in Thailand and Argentina, I read Scott Bessenecker's book, *The New Friars*, which told of Christian monks through the centuries who had lived in voluntary poverty, and modern-day people who were moving into *barrios*, slums, and *favelas* around the world to live in solidarity with the poor. A voice in my mind (I still believe this was the voice of God) told me very clearly as I read it, *This is going to be you.* The revelation both thrilled and terrified me. I sobbed, picturing what I imagined to be a lonely and difficult life. Who would be willing to do that with me? Certainly not my boyfriend of almost three years, who had lived his entire life in Texas and felt homesick every time he spent more than a week away. When I mentioned to another person for the first time my sense of calling, her response was that God "surely wouldn't ask me to do something so extreme."

The New Friars introduced me to an organization called Servants, which was essentially a network of Christian teams living in Asian slums and seeking out diverse ways of demonstrating God's love in their various contexts. Depending on the needs of their communities, they opened social businesses, or advocated for land rights, or ran homework clubs, or developed recovery programs for drug-addicted youth. But mainly they just lived life alongside their neighbors in poverty—befriending them, learning from them, and finding ways to show love, which usually meant finding ways to work alongside them to improve their lives.

Andy was the only person I knew who was crazy enough to take these ideas seriously, and we frequently spent hours on the phone together during those turbulent months of navigating culture shock with my family, boyfriend, and—it seemed to me at the time—all of American Christendom. I was angry about the foundational assumptions in my worldview that had turned out to be false and angry that everyone around me continued to live in middle-class ease without seeming to know or care about the ways they were entrenched in oppressive political and economic systems.

Back at university in the fall, it became increasingly clear that my now long-distance boyfriend and I were pursuing different futures, and I finally decided to end the relationship. Andy and I started dating shortly afterward. Initially, our dates were routinely interrupted by total strangers coming by to ask for change or food and then staying to tell their life stories, to which Andy would patiently listen without knowing how to extract himself. As an already-infatuated girlfriend, this characteristic only further charmed me, and we were both keen to build relationships with people on the streets. But we eventually learned that if we wanted guaranteed time alone together, we couldn't eat dinner at a restaurant with outdoor tables because of the way homeless people were magnetized by Andy's gentle, friendly aura.

Along with several friends, we dropped out of church and started spending more time with people we were certain would never feel comfortable inside the churches we attended—people like the ones who crashed our dinner dates. Though we hadn't completely shaken our evangelistic impulse, we were no longer satisfied with one-dimensional dogma and religious formulas. We didn't want people to just pray the sinner's prayer. We now believed that accepting Jesus was more about becoming friends with homeless people and building community and opposing violence and caring about the ways that our lifestyles were contributing to global injustice and inequality.

Then we went back to church, but an interracial church next door to projects in the inner city, where hardly anyone looked or sounded or acted like us, but the community was real and we felt vital and alive. My faith was broadening to include social justice and community rather than just personal relationship with God and spiritual salvation. But in many ways, my earliest religious training remained intact: I was learning a new definition of following Jesus, and yet guilt and fear remained subconscious motivations for the way I lived out my faith.

When Andy and I graduated from college, we were young and passionately in love—with one another, with God, and with our heady ideals. While the concept of intentional poverty had a ring of familiarity for Andy, whose family had experienced a degree of unintentional poverty during his missionary childhood, it was more of an exotic idea for me. My parents paid for my car insurance, my gas, and my college tuition, and I couldn't remember ever having had to worry about money. Though we were both sold on the idea of living in a slum, everyone we knew advised us against that undertaking during our first year of marriage. In fact, most people advised us against even moving overseas during our first year together. Nevertheless, we got married a few weeks after graduation and boarded a plane to Asia the next day to backpack our way through a six-week honeymoon in Vietnam. Then we traveled to the English teaching jobs in China that we had found online in a city we knew nothing about.

We spent our first year of marriage in that grimy, developing city, and we handled it: we spoke good Chinese;

we made local friends. We hosted parties and Bible studies in our apartment and discussed Jesus' subversive kingdom and his inversion of social hierarchy. So by age twenty-three, when we were applying to join Servants and planning our initial visit to India, we felt experienced and capable and ready for anything. We also thought that we had finished overhauling our theology and that we had things basically figured out. Most of our hard-and-fast certainties would not survive the journey that was to follow.

3

THE FIRST CALL

India, July–August 2011 and North America, September 2011–April 2012

On our first trip to India, Andy and I visited various cities in the north of the country, ending in Delhi, where there was already a Servants team living and working in a slum community. Our first stop was Kolkata, where we were mesmerized by the pulsing energy of the loud, crowded streets, and the riot of color that surrounded us in the form of textiles, flowers, and food. Our nostrils were assaulted with the unfamiliar smells of Bengali spices, incense being burned at thousands of temples and small shrines around the city, and—here and there—the stench of garbage rotting in the tropical sun. We drank hot, milky chai from clay cups at roadside stands and sitting on the floors of simple rooms in the slums. We also spent a few days volunteering at Mother Teresa's home for the destitute and dying, where we were moved by the compassion and the joyful energy of the Sisters of Charity as they tended to some of the most impoverished, neglected people in the city.

One morning, we went on a walking tour of the city and wound up handing out bread to people who were begging at Howrah train station. There, we met an elderly woman with a small, skinny child who began weeping, placing her feeble hand on mine and pouring out what I can only imagine was a heartfelt lament and an appeal for help—in a language we couldn't understand. I could only hold her hand and listen, not comprehending her words, but responding to the emotion behind them. We felt completely powerless. Another day at Mother Teresa's, a wizened old man who had just been brought in, caked in the mud of the streets and stiff with age and neglect, passed away while Andy bathed him. Days later, as we made our way to the clinic in the morning, we saw a train crush an American teenager, a short-term volunteer, damaging his leg so badly that it had to be amputated at the hip. He had been walking just a few feet behind us on a commuter train station platform when it happened, and Andy was one of the ones to pull his body out from under the undercarriage of the train afterwards. Kolkata struck us as a frightening place, where desperate people seemed to cling to life as it slipped through their hands like sand. We felt overwhelmed by the unnerving coexistence of life and death, growing alongside each other like twins in the womb. We had never seen such misery.

The morning we were to leave for Delhi, I woke up with a fire burning in my head and a man repeating "hello" into a microphone that must have been a block away but sounded like it was blasting from the foot of my bed. Throughout the morning, the thin walls and windows of the apartment where we were staying were assaulted by sound checks and then Hindu worship songs playing ceaselessly over loudspeakers on a two-song loop. To my unaccustomed ears, it was a nightmare of percussion and piercing soprano wails.

But after a dose of Advil, I was lucid enough for the taxi ride through festival day traffic to the train station, where we boarded the overnight train to Delhi. The next morning, we were met at the station by Michael, an Australian member of the Servants team, who had lived in the slums with his wife, Kat, and their two sons, for seventeen years.

Together, we rode in a beat-up taxi van to a densely populated "unauthorized" community of crude brick houses, small jeans factories, and dairy buffalo stables along dirt streets. We caused quite a scene unloading our large pieces of luggage and then walking along a narrow alleyway to the single room that Michael's family called home.

We were quickly at ease in their home, as the entire family was witty, down-to-earth, and comfortable in their own skin—not to mention incredibly nonchalant about sharing their small space with strangers for several days on end. Andy and I were visiting at the same time as a young woman from South Africa, who was also considering joining the team, so there were three of us living as guests in their tiny home. Their calm, collected dispositions were comforting in the midst of what was otherwise a completely unfamiliar situation. In sharp contrast to the Hinduism of Kolkata, this part of Delhi was a Muslim area, and the climate was more of a desert than a jungle, so it was almost hard to believe we were still in the same country.

When I ventured outside with Kat to buy vegetables at the market, the heat was a crushing weight, bearing down on me. I traversed a congested maze of pathways lined with towering brick walls, sweating under the headscarf I was wearing to blend in, and feeling slightly bitter about having to cover my head. Following closely behind Kat, I swam in a river of black veils, beards, crowds, cows, and vegetables, hardly able to focus my vision—let alone my mind. After we returned to the house, Kat took my temperature, and I discovered that I had a fever of 102 degrees Fahrenheit. I was relieved to have a fever because it meant that I wasn't as intolerant of the heat as I had thought. The slow burn that had enveloped my body since arriving was due to illness, not (exclusively) the climate.

That night, we unrolled the family's "table" and had dinner on the floor, sitting around a plastic mat laden with egg curry, rice, and chapatti. We slept on the family's flat roof under an open, desert sky, and awoke to the morning activity of their neighbors' morning routines: listening to music, bathing, playing, and hanging out on their roofs. Except for the Hindi film songs playing over cell phone speakers, the scene called to mind images of biblical Palestine: flat roofs, tethered goats, dusty roads, dark beards, and flowing traditional clothing.

The next day, Andy and I headed into the city to explore on our own. We passed Ba'hai, Sikh, and Hindu temples; mosques; ancient tombs and modern office buildings; historical palaces and shopping malls. We visited a Muslim neighborhood where pilgrims came to visit a saint's tomb and to bathe in the waters of a mystical pool said to have healing powers—not too different from the pool of Siloam mentioned in the New Testament, a place in first-century Judea whose waters were said to be stirred by angels on occasion, after which the first person into the pool would be healed of whatever ailed them. Then we wandered around an enclave of Tibetan refugees and sat in a coffee shop surrounded by Buddhist monks who had established a monastery in exile.

There was so much to take in: cows wandered the streets freely, and mongooses scampering along the ground were as common as the squirrels back in North America. At a public park, we walked in the shade of ancient *peepal* trees whose trunks were bundles of tangled vines exploding out of the earth and flowing into the air like torrents of water frozen into a wood carving. Monkeys and peacocks roamed beneath the magnificent spread of their branches. We also passed homeless grandmothers and children begging on the street, their hair bleached light-brown from malnutrition.

Delhi was a study in contrast, including the yawning gap between rich and poor. The metropolis boasted an extensive air-conditioned metro system, but such development ended at the exit gates. We would emerge from modern underground infrastructure onto pot-holed dirt roads lined with rickshaws, their drivers waiting to pedal us to our destination. Women in the slums covered their heads outdoors and spent most of their days indoors, washing, cooking, sewing, and cleaning the home. But the women on the metro wore jeans and talked on iPhones as they commuted to work. Middle-class Indians spoke English and studied at universities; poor Indians were illiterate.

With Andy's light eyes, blond hair, and red beard, he looked Kashmiri in some people's eyes. My dark hair, dark eyes, and olive coloring made me racially ambiguous, and I could sometimes pass as a light-skinned Indian. But the way we walked, gestured, and carried ourselves was foreign; when the two of us were together, the sum total of all these subtle differences made it obvious that we were not Indians. As a young foreign woman, I was of particular interest to local men, so I developed the habit of looking at the ground or staring vacantly ahead of me whenever I was outside, in order to avoid making eye contact with any of the men who would already be looking back at me. I wasn't at all sure that I wanted to live there.

As we wandered the city, we reflected on the inspiring lives of the people we had met who were living in the slums, and we wondered if we would join a Servants team in that difficult place. We had spent the past few weeks walking ankle-deep through floodwater to visit their homes, tagging along to visit their friends who lived on the edges of trash heaps, and drinking chai on the floor in their simple rooms, and we had been persuaded that this crazy life of voluntary poverty was not only possible, but also purposeful and rewarding. One of the Servants workers we met had explained to us how even an act as small as serving tea to guests could be subversive and "prophetic": he could declare the equality of the Kingdom of God by choosing to pour tea for women or younger people first, instead of following the local custom of serving the oldest male first and the youngest female last.

Andy and I believed in this Kingdom that Jesus had so often spoken of in the gospels. We were compelled by this vision of community and this way of being in the world, because it embodied what we understood to be God's desires for wholeness, justice, and loving communion between human beings and Himself. We believed that this upside-down Kingdom Jesus spoke of not only included the people who were most often left out in society, but that all of these marginalized people were honored with a central role in it. We believed that people who are poor, those with mental health issues or physical disabilities or addictions, the socially awkward, the unlikeable, the screw-ups, the weak, and the humble had much to teach the powerful, prideful people who so often occupied positions of influence and privilege in our world. We believed that in His love for all of humanity, God was especially concerned about the welfare of the most vulnerable people, because they needed more attention and help than those whose lives were already protected by wealth, education, and the civic institutions of the dominant culture.

But our decision to move into a slum was not merely a logical outworking of our understanding of Christianity, for we had felt very direct and personal invitations from God into this kind of life. So if we wanted to be faithful to our call, we had to make this work—no matter what. For these reasons, moving into a slum didn't feel like a radical choice so much as an exhilarating continuation of the trajectory our lives were already on. It was terrifying and exciting and many things in between, but mostly, it seemed inevitable. It was no longer a question of whether, but where, so if India was not the place for us, we assumed we would join Servants in another Asian slum instead.

A few days after our arrival in Delhi, Andy and I went to spend a week with a local host family, who were longtime friends and former neighbors of Michael and Kat. When Faisal, our host father, picked us up and took us to his home, he communicated in very limited English that we were welcome to stay with his family for a week, a month, or however long we wished. Such radical hospitality was the theme of our time with his family.

Soon after we arrived, Faisal's adult son told us, "Tell us frankly if you are hungry," which I think translated to, "Make yourself at home."

The first night with the family, we were given the option of sleeping at our host's house or at one of the two sisters' homes nearby. We shrugged and said we were happy to sleep anywhere. Immediately, the son announced matter-of-factly, "Andy, you will sleep on the roof."

Andy looked at him quizzically. "By myself?"

"Will you be lonely?" the son asked him.

Andy and I just looked at each other, unsure of what to do.

"Trudy, you sleep here."

I had been assigned to sleep with three of the sisters on the floor in another room. The next afternoon, we tactfully tried to revise our sleeping arrangement.

"Would it be alright if we slept at your sister's house tonight?" we asked the son.

He looked at us squarely. "You are not comfortable at our house," he stated.

"No, no, it's just . . . you know, we usually sleep together. We're married."

"Oh, I see," he replied. "You are habitual."

Yeah, I guess you could say that.

Andy and I laughed together about taking bucket showers on our family's front porch in a little shack, where I could see construction workers and door-to-door cloth salesmen through the cracks in the rough-hewn wooden door. We were humbled by our complete ignorance about how to accomplish the most basic tasks, such as laundry and cooking. We relaxed with our host family in the cool of the day, talking and watching the setting sun soak the sky in pink and orange as we listened to the evening call to prayer sung out across the rooftops from the mosque. The sisters drew henna tattoos onto the palms of my hands, dressed me up in an old wedding dress belonging to one of the sisters, made up my face beyond recognition with lipstick on my lips and my eyelids, and then stood back and said, "Gorgeous!"

As we began to form friendships with our new family—who had welcomed us into their world, sharing their food, space, and time with us—I began to believe that I could survive in India. Because I wasn't the domestic type and did not fit the role of a quiet, submissive female, the idea of spending the majority of my life inside was unthinkable. It also made me angry that I would have to cover my head with fabric in the desert heat while men walked around the neighborhood in their boxers. But as I talked with my host sisters and listened to their stories, my heart broke for their powerlessness and pain. As I faced my own fears and struggles about living in India, I marveled at their strength, creativity, and resilience. Though other Servants workers had talked about the prophetic power of taking on lifestyle "nuisances" in order to communicate the worth of people who were not valued by society, my Indian sisters themselves stirred me to live in such a way alongside them.

* * *

Following our visit to India, we spent almost nine months visiting family and friends across North America, fundraising, attending training, and living in community with another American couple in their thirties who, along with Michael and Kat and their two boys, would become our teammates in India. We spent a lot of time dreaming together about what our life would look like as a team.

As part of our preparation, Andy and I attended a two-week Servants orientation in Vancouver, Canada. Servants has a heavy theological and practical emphasis on living in solidarity with people in poverty. This meant that we would be living close to the level of the people were hoping to serve in India, both to emulate Jesus' decision to enter the world as one of us, and also because this would eliminate barriers to relationship with our neighbors. We were already committed to Servants' philosophy of partnering with people, entering into their experience, and learning from them in relationship in order to encourage community ownership of projects.

But in Vancouver, we realized that our decision to become good neighbors to those around us was not a black-and-white, either/or proposition, but rather one movement in a long journey toward solidarity and away from isolation. We were encouraged to see our relationships with others as dynamic, rather than static, and our decision to move toward solidarity as a gradual journey made up of countless small choices and actions over time. This journey would look different for each individual, depending on our culture, our personality, and our life situation. Thus relocating into a slum wouldn't guarantee a movement toward solidarity and away from isolation, since the experience of living in close proximity with others could create stress that might cause us to tune people out instead of remaining emotionally present and available to them. One of the facilitators at our orientation explained that if we were going to move toward others, we would need to choose on a regular basis to continue being emotionally vulnerable, available, and interruptible as we opened our homes and lives to others.

Though I nodded my head, I found it much easier to think of "solidarity" and "isolation" as two distinct categories—like the sheep and the goats in Matthew 25—rather than as a continuum. I was thrilled by the shiny, new ideals of solidarity, simplicity, nonviolence, community, empowerment, and servanthood—and I could eloquently explain their nature and importance. This was a time of anticipation, preparation, restlessness, and excitement, but I had no idea how much learning still lay ahead of me.

II.
UNRAVELING OF CERTAINTY

Spring 2012–Winter 2012

"You tell me you care about the poor. Then tell me, what are their names?"

—Gustavo Gutierrez

4
FINDING HOME

April–November 2012

Faisal's Family

Because we wanted to bond with local people and become comfortable in our host culture, rather than rely on an insular community of other foreigners to help us navigate through the period of adjustment to life in India, we and our Western teammates decided to spend our first weeks with host families rather than with each other. Once again, Andy and I moved in with Faisal's family.

Five times a day, the call to prayer rose from a loud-speaker. Five or six times a day, we drank chai with the family: tiny cups of steaming black tea loaded with milk and sugar. Throughout the day, we hung out on the front step to talk with people walking past, or to laugh at the baby water buffalo that lived in front of the house across the street. Sometimes, we would make a trip to the market with Faisal to buy vegetables, or to the huge community milk-vending machine marked with the words, "Mother

Dairy." In the afternoon, when it was hottest outside, most people took a nap, and we soon adopted this practice as well. In the evenings—after we had a bit of basic language—Andy and I went out to talk with neighbors and occasionally were invited to their homes for more chai. Dinner happened anytime between 8:30 and 10 o'clock at night, and after that we would sit around talking with our host sisters and brother. At around 11, we would head back to our room and then spend the next half hour chasing down the mosquitoes that had ended up on the inside of the mosquito netting that hung over the blankets we had spread out on the floor as our bed.

We found joy in becoming part of our Indian family's daily rhythms of work and relaxation, and it was a blessing to have a safe environment within their home to make our first cultural blunders. We were thankful to have advocates and friends who could help us integrate into the community. Yet there were times when the cultural gulf between us was perplexing.

One afternoon, Andy and I had been trying to take a nap when we were disturbed by yelling and screaming upstairs. We climbed the steps to see what was happening, and in the room directly opposite ours—just a few feet away from the railing of the balcony where we stood—we saw a woman throwing dishes and hitting her teenage daughter. After a few seconds, someone pulled a curtain across the open room, and we could only see figures and objects moving against the cloth, but the screaming and the sounds of blows falling continued for several minutes. One of our host sisters found us there on the balcony.

"Rehmat, what do we do?" We had asked frantically. "We have to do something! Can you ask her to stop?"

Rehmat furrowed her brow, looking worried, and tried to move us away from the balcony. But we stayed where we were, eyes fixed on the curtain across the alleyway.

Our host sister stood next to us, watching uncomfortably for a few more moments before finally shooing us away.

Later that afternoon, we brought up the incident with the rest of the family and were shocked when they began to laugh hysterically, making jokes and offering comedic reenactments of the scene.

Overwhelmed, I began to cry. "I don't understand," I told them. "I didn't think it was funny at all."

The women in the room immediately grew serious as, one after the other, they explained that they knew it wasn't funny. Abruptly, some of them also began to cry. Our host mother, Shazia, began to speak fervently in Hindi through her tears, and one of her daughters translated her words into English for us.

"This also makes us sad," she explained, "but what can we do? We see it all the time, but there is nothing we can do about it." As she related memories of her own powerlessness in the face of violence, I realized that each woman in the room had experienced enough suffering in life to make her pessimistic about being able to do much to change it.

Other interactions with our Indian family challenged our preconceived ideas about faith and religion. When we arrived at Faisal's home, two of our host sisters were pregnant. Shazia told us that both had been struggling to conceive children for several years without success, and so she had made a religious pilgrimage to a large *mazar* at Ajmeer in Rajasthan. Ajmeer is highly renowned across India as a place where prayers for physical healing and other miracles are certain to be answered. At Ajmeer, Shazia asked God to open her daughter's wombs—either by praying directly to the Muslim saint buried at Ajmeer, or by asking him to intercede on their behalf (it was unclear which). Within a week of her returning home, both women were pregnant.

Andy and I weren't sure what to make of that story. We had the vague notion that God's miraculous intervention was somehow limited to Christians, or at least to a Christian framework. Non-believers could certainly be healed, but wouldn't it always be through prayers to Jesus and through situations that fell into line with the specific precedents of Scripture? The free-flowing supernatural power Shazia described was outside the bounds of what we believed to be God's *modus operandi*, and it didn't fit into our worldview.

But the tangible experience of our new sisters challenged us to find a way to expand our perspective rather than sit in denial of such compelling proof of God's answer to Muslim prayers offered up through Muslim saints at a Muslim holy site. Although we didn't understand it, we chose to believe the family's story.

Who was I to decide how far the boundaries of God's love extended? And how could I even begin to categorize my non-Christian sisters as non-believers, when their fervent devotion to God and their faith in His love and power had led them to ask for this miracle in the first place? We later encountered some missionaries who would have attributed this apocryphal healing to demonic power, but our host family gave all the credit—and the gratitude—to God. The new babies assured them of God's loving interest in the details of their lives, so we couldn't see anything but good coming out of their prayers or their faith in God's power to heal.

Around the same time, I met Anisa, a beautiful twelve-year-old girl with a slight frame, a wide smile, and big, shining eyes. She often came over to Kat and Michael's house to play games with their two boys or to ask for fruit. She knew that there was usually a bowl overflowing with mangos, bananas, or whatever was in season at our teammates' house, and food was often in short supply in her own home.

Anisa's eyes lit up with excitement the day she arrived to find an intriguing batch of new foreigners sitting around the room. Upon hearing that I didn't speak any Hindi, she immediately set about teaching me the basics. But after a few unsuccessful attempts to get me to introduce myself properly in Hindi, Anisa gave up on verbal communication and moved on to a more effective medium: dance. She taught me a few Bollywood steps, and we laughed and danced together around the room as she hummed a Hindi song.

Anisa's situation disturbed me. She was so young, and yet so much of her life already seemed written in stone. She wasn't going to school. She seemed destined for early marriage and lifelong poverty, just like her parents. I was also thinking about her religion. *What would become of her if she never heard of Jesus?* I wondered. For that matter, what would happen to the thousands of other children like her in that one neighborhood alone? It didn't seem fair that the circumstances into which a person was born should determine so much about their lives, much less their eternal destinies. Was my salvation just another happy accident in the genetic lottery that had landed me in the Christian West?

When I voiced some of these unsettling thoughts over a meal, Michael's response surprised me. "Out of sixty thousand people in this slum, we're the only Christians we know of," he said. "It doesn't seem right that everyone here besides us could really be damned. It offends the conscience. It's a horrific idea. I don't even think the people who say they believe in hell *actually* believe the vast majority of the world is headed for eternal, conscious torment. Or if they do, they must be incredibly callous not to be doing a thing about it. It's easy enough to believe all non-Christians are going to hell when everyone you know and love is a Christian, but that view just doesn't hold up with the concept of God's love or justice once you start befriending people who are already living in hell on earth, who are supposedly damned afterwards, too."

It surprised me to learn that Michael's convictions as a Christian had led him to live among the Muslim poor, even though he didn't believe they were in danger of hell. I had come to India out of loving concern, but with the notion that part of my purpose there would be to convert people from their religious background to faith in Jesus. Wouldn't that be the only way for them to find meaning in their lives, or to experience peace and joy after they died? Michael's words poked holes in my assumptions, challenging the logic and the justice behind them. I didn't know what to do with these uncomfortable ideas, but I was unable to refute or dismiss them.

Yet our daily life did not provide much space to wrestle with these existential questions that disturbed my spiritual equilibrium, because we were so busy learning the language and culture, as well as the daily tasks of survival: where to buy vegetables and how to cook them; how to bargain for cloth at the market and where to have it sewn into clothes. As we tried to adjust to life in India, we continued to look for a city and a slum that our team would call home.

Manoj

After a few weeks with Faisal's family, Andy and I rented a room of our own in the same community where our teammates lived. Our landlord, Manoj, was also an unlikely transplant to the slum, since he was a high-caste Hindu man in his mid-thirties from a small town in the mountains. He had mysteriously ended up in the middle of a low-caste Muslim community in the plains, where he ran a successful photo studio. As best we could make out, there had been conflict with his strict religious parents, and he preferred living in relative freedom in the slum to enjoying opulence under his parents' roof. In general, he didn't seem to trust his Muslim neighbors and considered himself an outsider among them. Even so, he had a couple of close Muslim friends, and he took advantage of his independence to eat meat enthusiastically on a daily basis. (Muslims in India are hearty beef-eaters; his parents were religiously vegetarian.)

Manoj's friendly eagerness, his easy smile, and the seriousness with which he went about even the smallest tasks of hospitality were childlike and endearing. His photo studio was on the ground floor, his room was up an impossibly narrow flight of stairs on the second floor, and our room was on the third floor. Not being particularly poor himself, Manoj kept a washing machine in our nine-by-ten-foot room, where he continued to do laundry once a week, and on the level above our room, where we bathed and used a toilet in a tiny outhouse, the exhaust pipe from the air-conditioner installed in his room blew hot air onto what was already a very hot roof.

He and Andy would often chat while bathing on the roof in their underwear in the mornings (men in India often bathe, work, or lounge around in their underwear in or near their homes), and Manoj was keen to practice his limited English with us whenever possible. Over time, we learned that he had a wife and a young daughter, both of whom lived in his parents' home. It was evident from the way he talked and the pictures he showed us that he adored his daughter, whom he spoke with daily on the phone. So Andy and I were shocked when Manoj told us without hesitation that if his daughter ever married someone from a low caste, he would kill her. The strength of his conviction unnerved us, and it seemed out of place in his gentle character.

That was one of our first lessons in understanding an honor-based culture and the ways in which kind, loving, psychologically normal people could be steeped in an ideology that demanded the murder of one's own children for the preservation of something larger and more important than any individual: family and caste honor. Killing one's own daughter for her choice of husband would be a despicably evil action, but Manoj was not an evil person. It was perhaps the first time we had so clearly seen the separation between an ideology and the individual people who subscribed to it.

Ilahabad

Determined to move into the neediest slum we could find—yet where we could still survive—our small band of pilgrims spent the next few months wandering by train and on foot, looking for a city and a slum in North India that we could call home. Finally, by October, we had decided on a city: Ilahabad. Each family on our team would move into a different slum community, but we would all live near one another.

After regularly visiting the same neighborhood for three weeks to ask about rooms for rent, Andy and I finally found a ground-floor space with a door opening directly onto the alleyway—just what we wanted—and a landlord who wasn't intimidated by the prospect of taking us to the police to register us as new tenants. (Because we were foreigners, we were supposed to register with the local police wherever we took up residence.)

The slum where we wanted to live was a crowded cluster of small houses spreading back from the main road along the bank of a foul, blackened drainage canal. It had begun as a squatter community on government land and was yet to be authorized by the municipality, meaning that the government did not provide running water or electricity. Furthest from the canal, there were simple brick homes—some with solid roofs and some covered with plastic tarps, corrugated tin, or sheets of asbestos composite. As you moved closer to the canal, the homes deteriorated. Along the dirt pathway skirting the edge of the sludgy water, there was a row of bamboo and plastic shacks. Together, all these dwellings comprised a community of about 3,500 people.

Gita

Our landlady, Gita, was loud, forceful, impatient with our less-than-perfect Hindi comprehension, and difficult to communicate with because of her rapid, slurred speech (which we later learned was a village dialect spoken with a slight speech impediment). At the police station, she explained to the room filled with big, burly men in uniform that she had come to fill out paperwork for two foreigners who wanted to rent a room from her. As soon as she mentioned the name of the slum, the policemen threw their heads back and roared with laughter, ridiculing her for thinking that any white-skinned foreigners would want to live in a place as "bad" as that.

Finally Gita became exasperated and flung her arms toward us. "You tell them!"

We explained that we wanted to live in the slum to learn Hindi, because we knew that we would learn very quickly with so many people around. It took a moment for the police to recover from their surprise that we spoke their language, but once they had taken in the fact, they emphatically talked over each other to tell us how terrible the place was.

"One hundred percent of the people who live there are thieves." "At night there is so much drinking and fighting." "You won't be safe there." "We all speak Hindi. You can come here to the police station every day and learn from us." They went on to suggest wealthy neighborhoods in the city where we should live instead. We patiently explained, amid peals of laughter, that we had already looked all over the city and that Gita's neighborhood was where we felt most welcomed. We assured them that we had already visited many times and had eaten in people's homes, and we weren't afraid to live there. When their skepticism continued, we told them that we wanted to try it out, and if things turned out badly, we could leave.

A female officer who was standing in the doorway, listening to the commotion, threw up her hands as if to say, "If the foreigners want to do this crazy thing, we should let them. It's just their way."

"Come," one of the higher-ups relented. The whole crowd followed us into another room, where laughter gave way to more serious attempts to reason with us.

Finally, we turned to humor to move things along. "If we don't move into that room, then we'll just have to live here," Andy declared.

A grey-headed officer stared back at him from the other end of the table until laughter slowly spread around the room, and he finally cracked a smile.

When an officer told us to return the next day, Gita dramatically grabbed his arm. "Look," she pleaded. "These two have been wandering around for fifteen days now looking for a room, and they haven't found any. And this week they keep coming to me and they won't leave me alone until I let them move into this room. They are making me lose my mind! For my sake, just give us the form!"

After more laughter, the form appeared, but the superior officer flapped it around as he issued one final warning. "In my opinion, it is NOT a good place. You should not go outside after 8 p.m. You should not go inside anyone else's home."

We nodded, wondering if he had ever set foot in the neighborhood, much less visited at night. Finally, he sighed and signaled for another man to help Gita with the form, since she could neither read nor write. Then they helped us with our part of the form, since we were not yet literate in Hindi.

After pasting our photos onto the document and declaring us registered, the amused and incredulous crowd of police invited us to come back to the station to hang out. "It's like a big party here, every day!" One of the police-women showed me family photos and invited us to her wedding. Several officers offered to visit us once we were settled.

* * *

For the first few days after we moved into our new community, children and adults visited our room constant-ly, giving us suggestions on how to set things up, watch-ing to see how we would make food, and asking us how much we paid for each thing we brought home from the market. We had usually paid too much, which they always let us know.

Slowly, we learned how much we should bargain things down at the market, how to knead dough for *roti* with the perfect ratio of water to flour, and which spices to crush together for a meat dish. Our days were extremely full with visiting neighbors, and our minds were full of new words and unfamiliar names to memorize.

In between the hours of conversation, we set up our living space, but it was days before we were finally able to bathe, because we had to wait for the fresh layer of con-crete Gita's husband had put into our showering area to dry. Before that little improvement project, the corner of the room that served as our bathing space and kitchen sink had been unusable, because the water collected in the middle of the concave cement platform instead of draining into the little sewage trench outside. The same day we bathed for the first time in our new home, we also in-stalled a small plastic faucet at the base of our water storage drum in order to have some semblance of "running" water.

There was no indoor plumbing in the whole neighborhood. Our water came from a nearby bore well and was delivered to our water drum once a day from a plastic hose attached to a neighbor's motorized water pump. Every morning, that leaky hose was passed from house to house on our alley, and everyone paid the owner of the jet pump a small fee each month for water. At filling time, other plastic hoses in various states of decay crisscrossed the alleys of the slum, patched here and there with small, plastic bags tied around the holes where leaks had become particularly dramatic. During the hot season, water came twice a day, in the evenings as well as the mornings. For the rest of the day, we used the water from our drum for cooking, bathing, and laundry, and we ran some through our ceramic candle filter for drinking.

As we filled our water drum from the leaky hose every morning, we watched women and children from the waterfront alleyway haul water back and forth by hand in small containers. There was no morning hose service to their homes, and they were too close to the sewage canal to dig a well. When we headed over to Gita's back courtyard to use the outhouse, we looked over a low wall into that unpaved lane where we knew that there were no toilets at all.

Because of all the small interactions inherent in daily survival, we quickly met the people who lived around us and came to know their families and their stories. Many of those stories involved loss, and we were amazed by our neighbors' resiliency in the face of tragedy and death. We were also struck by the strength of the families in our community and their ability to care for the orphans, elderly, and vulnerable among their relatives. We met an extended family who cared for their orphaned relative (a one-year-old girl whose father had run away after her mother died in childbirth) and a single mother who had taken a job as hired help in a rich family's home to be able to keep sending her children to school.

For the next several months, Andy spent a lot of time wandering around with the men in our neighborhood, drinking chai and visiting their workplaces: collection stands for recyclables, motorcycle repair places, a work-shop directly opposite our room where several skilled craftsmen made beautiful, wooden furniture by hand. None of those jobs were well-paid. There were several furniture factories nearby, which employed teenagers and boys as young as eight to do the tedious, dirty work of spray-painting metal cabinets or sanding furniture for hours each day without masks or any other safety precau-tions. But most of the men in the community had no per-manent job location. They were *kabadi walle*, recycling collectors, who pedaled flat-bed, three-wheeled rickshaws around wealthy neighborhoods calling out, *"Kabadiiiiiii! Kabadi-adi-ooo!"* Their livelihood was dependent on oth-er people generating waste. It was highly seasonal, accord-ing to when the weather permitted them to spend the day pedaling around, and when people were getting rid of old things.

I spent a lot of time visiting women in their homes, where many of them were hidden away from the outside world because of cultural tradition, a conservative mother-in-law, or fear of sexual harassment. Though the threat of harassment had basis in reality, it was often trumped up and used as a means of control. For months after moving into the neighborhood, Andy never saw many of my friends because they weren't allowed to leave the house. And when I passed the men that he knew during the course of the day, they usually ignored me for the sake of propriety, since it was inappropriate for them to greet a young woman on the street. But together, we could visit the families who lived in crowded plastic and bamboo tents on the alley behind our room, several feet lower and closer to the black river that sometimes flooded their homes during monsoon.

As we came to know our slum, we realized that it was made up almost entirely of migrants from nearby villages. Though they had lived for decades in the city, they still considered their home to be somewhere in the countryside. Because so many people had been forced to leave the villages for work over the years, most of our neighbors were blood relatives. New migrants tended to settle near family members who were already established, so the whole settlement was made up of virtually two or three large clans.

When asked, "Where do you live?" many of our neighbors replied that they "lived" in the village they had come from, and they used the Hindi term *gumna* to describe what they had been doing in the city for the past fifteen or twenty years. *Gumna* means to wander, travel, or go somewhere temporarily—literally, "to move in circles."

For many people, urban living was a necessary evil because there was not enough work or land to sustain them in the countryside. We caught glimpses of our neighbors' village roots in their habit of waking with the sun, their obliviousness to clock time, their penchant for walking around barefoot. Their rural background was obvious in their love for raising goats, ducks, chickens, and even cows, and—especially among some of the men—in their preference for attending to the calls of nature outside, even if there was a toilet available.

Some of the poorest families we met, people who were living in tiny hovels made of rice bags sewn together over a skeleton of bamboo sticks, had previously lived in large houses that served as extended family compounds in the village. Some of them even owned land. But the land wasn't producing enough to sustain them all, so they had been forced to give up their ancestral homeland and the wholesome goodness of wide-open spaces to come and scrape out their survival in a crowded, dirty, urban settlement.

In the face of all this adversity, however, our neighbors were incredibly resilient and creative. They found ways to survive despite the odds and the unjust power stacked against them. There's a word in Hindi to describe the kind of highly pragmatic, resourceful problem-solving that we saw our neighbors using from day to day: *jugaad*. An English speaker might call it "jerry-rigging," or use "MacGyver" as a verb to approximate the same meaning, but there's really no English equivalent for the broad scope of this quintessentially Indian skill.

Jugaad was a teenage boy plugging a leak in our water drum by scraping off pieces from a waxy bar of soap and applying it to the hole in the plastic like putty.

Jugaad was a man somehow making a living by painting monkeys as leopards and peddling them through residential neighborhoods as entertainment.

Jugaad was a family opening a restaurant even though they didn't have a building, a sink, or a stove, keeping up with business by cooking over a wood fire inside of a handmade mud oven, and seating customers under the same tarp that sheltered the whole family at night.

Jugaad was leaving the plugs off of electrical wires so that five appliances could be powered by sticking the exposed metal ends into a single outlet.

Basically, *jugaad* was finding a way to accomplish what was necessary in spite of any logistical, natural, or bureaucratic barrier that presented itself. In our little village in the city, we came to appreciate how people survived on the determined, implausible, ingenious improvisation of *jugaad* every day.

* * *

When Andy and I moved into the slum, it suddenly felt like we were living with about 3,500 people, and we could hear them all around us: traffic; neighbors' voices through the walls; sitar and drums blaring out from someone's cell phone as they walked past our room playing music from the latest Hindi film; people calling "*Hut! Hut!*" to shoo cows away from their doors; children's laughter; the banging of hammers and grinding of saws in the wood shop across the alley. These were some of the sounds that greeted us when we first opened our eyes under the mosquito net in the morning. Our community was a noisy place, and the longer we lay in bed in the morning, the more sounds joined the chorus. Sometimes we loved all the noise, and other times it drove us crazy, but either way the cacophony reminded us that we were not alone—there was a lot of life going on around us, and we were connected to it all.

As I reflected on our budding friendships within our new community, I thought of the story recorded in Luke chapter 10, when Jesus is cross-examined by an expert in Jewish religious law who wants to know what he must do to "enter into life." The man's mind is probably on the complex purity codes and ritual protocols, but Jesus directs him back to the same words he has already read hundreds of times in the Hebrew Scriptures: "Love the Lord your God with all your heart and with all your soul and with all your strength and with all your mind," and, "Love your neighbor as yourself."[2] Because the legal expert wanted to engage in a theological debate with Jesus, he is disappointed with such a simple response, and so he searches for a way to make things more complicated—and

---

[2] Deuteronomy 6:5, Luke:10:27

to relieve himself of responsibility. "Who is my neighbor?" he asks.

After a few weeks of our "dorm life" experience in the slum, this man's question struck us as odd. We regularly heard the arguments between families. We knew who was looking for a job and who had found one, whose baby was sick, and whose relative had died. Waiting in line for the outhouse together, sharing laundry line space, talking at the doorway and through the walls, eating together, experiencing the rain and the power outages and the festivals together—we could never wonder who our neighbors were! We often failed at loving our neighbors as ourselves (particularly the ones with whom we shared the closest quarters), but our lives were so intertwined with theirs that the scribe's question seemed absurd.

His question reveals that he was living in isolation from people—and their needs—and so he could look around without seeing any "neighbors" at all. If we put enough walls and busyness between ourselves and the people around us, we will become oblivious to their needs and joys, and we will fail to recognize them as neighbors.

Sometimes community life felt like two steps forward, one step back—or one step forward and two steps back—but we continued to stumble on, because we were convinced of the beauty of the life we felt Jesus calling us into.

5

A SLIVER OF LIGHT IN THE DARKNESS

December 2012–July 2013

"There is in all things an inexhaustible sweetness and purity, a silence that is a fount of action and joy. It rises up in wordless gentleness and flows out to me from the unseen roots of all created being, welcoming me tenderly, saluting me with indescribable humility. This is at once my own being, my own nature, and the Gift of my Creator's Thought and Art within me, speaking as Hagia Sophia, speaking as my sister, Wisdom."

—Thomas Merton, "Hagia Sophia"

Just two days before Christmas, Andy and I participated in a protest march in downtown Ilahabad after a young woman on a bus in Delhi was brutally attacked and gang-raped, and later died from her injuries. As women in India had begun to assert their right to inhabit public spaces alongside men, instances of rape had also risen, and this most recent crime aroused national outrage and a public cry for justice.

As we marched through Ilahabad with our candles alight in the cold dusk, I thought about the pain and terror that the woman had endured, the grief and shock of her family, and the trauma shared by so many other victims who had not been wealthy or important enough to garner the media's attention. I thought about all the women in my neighborhood who were suffering violence on a regular basis, and yet were not able to take part in this protest because of the strict traditions of male control that governed their lives.

As we marched, our flickering, vulnerable flames reminded me of Isaiah 42:3: "A bruised reed he will not break, and a smoldering wick he will not snuff out" ("...till he leads justice to victory"[3]). I had long known that this passage described Jesus, but our time in the slum was revealing more of Jesus' vulnerability and fragility—I saw that He Himself was that bruised reed and smoldering wick. Even though He had been stripped, tortured, and killed by the powers of evil in his day, His Kingdom was continuing to come through the weakness of human beings who often failed or were overpowered by colossal systems of injustice and evil.

In describing His own life and the lives of those who would follow in His footsteps, Jesus used the image of a kernel of wheat. He said that unless the kernel falls to the ground and dies, it will remain a single seed. But when a seed dies, it nurtures new life, which is multiplied over and over again, symbolizing the paradox of resurrection.[4]

Our candlelight procession also reminded me of the gospel of John: "The light shines in the darkness, but the darkness has not overcome it."[5] And yet as we walked

---

[3] Matthew 12:20

[4] John 12:24

[5] John 1:5

through the streets, bearing our tiny lights in the darkness, I reflected that thus far, the light had not yet been able to overcome the darkness. As I focused on the bright light from my candle, the surrounding shadows grew darker, and I thought about how our life of following Jesus often felt like this candlelight vigil in the dark. Even though the darkness was diminished by the presence of our candles, their feeble light could never completely dispel the darkness. Only the sunrise could do that.

Yet it seemed to me in those somber moments of remembrance and resistance at the march that Jesus' life was a flame of truth given to light our path through the darkness. And in following Him, we could walk in that light, offering our own lives as fragile, flickering candles, burning with love through the night with the desperate hope that dawn would come and the shadows of violence, evil, and confusion would recede once and for all. As I marched with those dozens of other tiny light-bearers, I raised my candle and renewed my commitment to throw in my lot with the Bruised Reed who could not be broken, the Smoldering Wick who lit the world on fire.

* * *

We rang in the New Year on a cold railway platform in the middle of the night, waiting for an 11 p.m. train which finally arrived at 2 a.m. A night on the rails and an all-day bus ride later, we found ourselves in a small town in the hills of central India, where we spent the next four days praying, resting, and venturing out on nature hikes in the wild. The sunny days under the big blue dome of the sky were a welcome reprieve from the cold, grey days in the slum, where low-hanging clouds formed a low ceiling over the rising smoke of the plastic and wood fires our neighbors lit to keep warm.

The rape in Delhi and the unfolding traumas of our neighbors had hollowed out our souls with sadness, and we were tired of clinging to hope while we lived in the tension of so many questions about God's presence in the midst of all of it all. Did He witness the savage attack onboard that bus? Did God have the power to act? If so, then why didn't He intervene? If not, then what good was this powerless God, anyway?

As I sat in the garden of the small monastery where we were staying, surrounded by trees, flowers, and birds, I reflected on God's vulnerability—how He had opened Himself up to rejection and humiliation—and how He had *submitted* to humanity by entering into our world as a human, emptying Himself of power, operating on our level, and eventually allowing Himself to be misunderstood, mistreated, brutalized, and killed. For a long time, I had struggled with questions about God's power, but on this retreat I began to meditate on the mystery of God's vulnerability, tenderness, and receptivity—and I realized these apparent weaknesses were not shortcomings, but were central to the way of love and therefore at the heart of how God worked in the world.

Rather than making demands and exerting control, God worked through relationship, patience, and compassionate invitation. Jesus demonstrated this strength-in-weakness through his humble self-sacrifice. During those days of quiet reflection, I felt the nurturing, mothering presence of God, and I was struck by how those aspects of God's nature were expressed in the fragile beauty of the natural world and also in the feminine half of humanity.

For so long, I had struggled with my identity as a female in the midst of a society that oppressed women. I was bitter about the way that the female body has been commodified as a sexual object for male consumption, and angry that feminine beauty had invited such widespread abuse. I had seen for myself how in India—as in so much of the world—being beautiful is a liability rather than an asset, especially among poor women. I had grown frustrated by my inability to find a single culture or ideology that offered a template for human sexuality which did not seem to somehow degrade women. I realized that I resented God for creating women as beautiful and vulnerable.

During these meditations, I sensed a revelation growing within me: my vulnerability and beauty as a woman were reflections of the image of God. Jesus Himself was vulnerable. And the very things which made Him attractive—His absolute freedom from others' opinions, His compassion, His humility, and His courage in speaking the truth—drew others to Him and also incited His enemies to kill Him. Like so many poor women that I knew in India, His beauty invited abuse. Though He wasn't raped, He was crucified.

As I reflected further, I was struck by how the language I used to refer to God typically reflected only the masculine aspects of the Divine nature—strength, power, and protection—without adequately describing the feminine aspects of mystery, or of birthing new life and new possibilities into the world. Growing up, I had been taught to relate to God as male, and I began to wonder if our habit of describing God in masculine language reinforced our societal tendency to devalue the feminine experience. I also wondered if masculine language served to make women feel more distant from or fearful of God. The women I knew in my community were unguarded and unselfconscious about their bodies when they were with other women, but in front of men, they felt the need to cover themselves. The way they covered their heads during prayer was similar: propriety, rather than intimacy, was the priority. They were approaching *Him,* after all.

Of course, many women told me that they wore the *niqab*, a veil covering all but a woman's eyes, as a way of identifying themselves as Muslims. And one friend told me that she covered her head in public simply because, "This is what our people wear." Some women equated modesty with personal dignity, which struck me as a healthy alternative to the idea that one must earn worth by putting her body on display for the inspection and approval of others. Yet other women wore the veil to avoid scrutiny in public. I had even considered wearing the *niqab* myself because I had grown tired of men's staring and harassment.

But I also knew women whose husbands or in-laws forced them to cover their faces in front of their fathers-in-law or to wear the full *niqab* outside as an oppressive tactic of control. My friends also told me that many men interpreted nontraditional clothing as an invitation to sexually harass women. I heard this myself after the Delhi rape, when many of the men in our community blamed the victim by saying that she must have caused the attack by dressing inappropriately or being out late at night.

In a similar way, modesty codes had been enforced on me and my peers when we were young girls at church camp. We had internalized a sense of shame and suspicion toward our bodies as something from God. In my mainstream Western culture—just as in India—lust was not seen as a male problem, but an inevitable response to female flesh. But was God really just another "male," who—along with the men and boys at church—required our modesty and submission in order to avoid objectifying women and using them for His own gratification?

Though I knew that the English language lacked a personal pronoun that could fully capture God's essence, I felt drawn to begin using feminine language to refer to God in order to challenge my ingrained bias toward a masculine view of God. In Hindi, this gender dichotomy is avoided altogether, because the personal pronouns for *he* and *she* are the same, but as I began to refer to God with feminine language in English, my relationship with God began to shift. When I felt angry about the ways women were mistreated by male-dominated systems, I invited God to nurture me as a mother. Pouring out my heart to *Her* reminded me that God is able to relate fully to my experience as a woman, and that deepened my sense of trust, safety, and receptivity to the Spirit's voice within me.

* * *

Though Andy and I prepared to return to our home in the slum with renewed energy to face the plight of our poor neighbors, we were assaulted by suffering before we arrived home. While waiting on another cold train platform, we stumbled across a baby who was lying helplessly on the cold station floor. Inches from the infant, a shop owner was selling snacks and bottled water to other passengers, and so we asked him where the baby had come from. He waved nonchalantly toward an empty area of the platform and said that the baby belonged to someone "over there." When we realized that the man had no idea who the parents were or where they had gone, we took the shivering infant into our arms.

When we picked up the baby, other bystanders began to offer information about a "husband and wife problem" and an argument during which a couple had left the baby and gone outside. Many people had witnessed the incident while they bought snacks, sold bottled water, or sat waiting for their trains on the platform. A moment later, a woman in a *sari* came hurrying down the platform.

"Oh, that's her," the shop keeper said, waving vaguely in her direction.

As the woman approached us, I could see blood flowing down the side of her head. In speechless shock, I handed her the baby. The woman avoided my gaze by lowering her head, then wordlessly took the baby and walked back across the platform.

"Yes, husband and wife problem," said a man standing nearby.

"No," I retorted. "Husband problem." I felt sickened by the lack of compassion for the mother or child.

Back home, we found our community much as we left it, except the weather had grown much colder. Though it was a stark contrast from the monastery in the hills, we saw beauty in the warm welcome of our neighbors, the children's excitement at our return, and an invitation to drink hot chai around an open fire in our friends' room.

***

By February, spring had arrived in its balmy, 80-degree glory, and full-fledged summer followed closely on its heels. In July, the teenage daughter of a Hindu family in our neighborhood went missing. I heard the rumors flying across doorways and carried by gleeful children through the alleys as I made my way home from the vegetable market:

She ran away with a boy. Her parents' noses will be cut off! That last phrase is an unnerving literal translation of a Hindi idiom meaning that a person will be shamed. I was confused.

When I had asked one of my neighbors about her disappearance, the young woman told me, "Yes, the daughter of the Hindus who run the dairy! She eloped."

"How do you know?" I pressed.

"Everybody says so," she replied nonchalantly.

"You shouldn't spread that story," I said with irritation. "We don't know what's happened. And that girl could be in danger."

My neighbor only shrugged. The community seemed to have reached consensus about the issue. The scandal was a source of entertainment.

Andy and I didn't know the family well. We had bought fresh buffalo milk from their dairy a few times, but we had only interacted with the sons who tended the herds. That evening we went to visit the family to find out if there was anything we could do to help with the search for their daughter. They welcomed us into a small room, where we joined the parents and older brother on their *taakat.* The girl's mother was a middle-aged woman in a *sari* with graying hair and teary eyes, her shoulders slumped with grief. Her father was white-haired and bare-chested in a cotton *dhoti,* his face creased with worry.

They handed us a photo of the missing girl. "She's fourteen years old," they told us. "We've been looking for her all over the city for days, and we are worn out—wandering everywhere on foot. We even went to the police, but they refused to help us."

We were confused to learn that their daughter had already been gone for several days. Why had it only become known today? Still, we were infuriated that the police were unconcerned and uncooperative. We promised to help in any way we could. Over the next few days, we took the parents to see a Catholic nun who was trained as a lawyer and ran a legal aid service. We accompanied the girl's father to meet with our friends, whose anti-trafficking organization began an investigation with the police. We prayed that the girl would come home safely. We saw the parents frequently, and they continued to update us with potential leads about their daughter.

They had heard a girl's screams coming from inside the house of a wealthy man who lived nearby, but servants had chased them away before they had a chance to investigate. The father somehow procured the cell phone number of his daughter's former classmate at school, a girl who apparently lived in a nearby slum and was known to have abandoned her studies a few years earlier to join her mother in working as a prostitute at the train station.

We feared the worst: trafficking, prostitution, murder. Such stories were not uncommon, and we had heard secondhand about underground red-light districts and organized crime operating in the city. We had Indian friends who partnered with police to raid brothels, and we passed on information about the missing girl's prostituted classmate in hopes that she, too, might be rescued.

One day, as we picked our way across the muddy yard of the dairy and skirted the flanks of the water buffalo standing in their stalls, the missing girl's father announced that he had news. His wife was standing in a corner, facing away from us. She circled incense in front of a small shrine as she sang in a strained voice, sniffing back tears.

"Today someone called us on a neighbor's phone—a boy. He said, 'I am your daughter's husband.'"

Andy and I were shocked and confused, but the parents seemed grimly unsurprised.

Police traced the call and accompanied the family to the small town from which it had come. The girl was returned home to her family; her husband, who was probably still a minor himself, was taken to jail.

In order to prevent another escape, the family forbade the daughter from leaving the house, and then they set about trying to marry her off as soon as possible.

"Isn't she too young to get married?" we asked.

But the family changed their estimation of her age. "Well, she's not really fourteen. Probably closer to sixteen, or eighteen."

Their meaning was clear: though she was forbidden to choose a spouse for herself, she was old enough to be forced into marrying a stranger.

When I discussed this bewildering series of events a few weeks later with a friend who worked at a local women's rights organization, she told me that alleging kidnapping is often the first port of call for families who are trying to drag their daughters back from unsanctioned marriages. The strange and confusing episode in our neighborhood turned out to be a routine case of a family trying to save face by controlling their daughter's choices—exactly the kind of case that discourages police from taking young girls' disappearances seriously.

Andy and I had done everything possible to help our distraught neighbors find their daughter, but in retrospect we realized we had been on the wrong side of the whole thing. The reason the family had waited for several days to approach the authorities about their missing daughter was that they had suspected her elopement from the beginning, and they had wanted to keep the whole thing quiet. Their daughter's safety and happiness were secondary to her family's honor.

***

As the heat of our second summer in India gave way to the rains of the monsoon season, I continued to reflect on the mystery of Christ living as a flame amidst the darkness of the world—and how our hope in Him continues to burn with that flickering light. Our hope is never quite strong enough to fill the room, but as long as Christ continues to burn within us, that hope will never cease. I often still felt that my hope was a lonely and feeble candle. But at other times, I had the sense that I was not only bearing a small flame in the darkness, but that I was a small sliver of a much greater light that had been painted over with temporary darkness. And as we worked to uncover more and more of that light, we would discover that the darkness, convincing as it might be, was only on the surface, whereas that great light was brilliant, permanent, and strong.

6

AMNA

Fall 2012–Fall 2013

"Seeking the face of God in everything, everyone, all the time, and his hand in every happening; this is what it means to be contemplative in the heart of the world. Seeing and adoring the presence of Jesus, especially in the lowly appearance of bread, and in the distressing disguise of the poor."

—Mother Teresa

We first met Amna, a conservative, middle-aged, Muslim woman who lived down the alley, during *Bakra Eid*— a big festival during which Muslims celebrate the story of God providing a goat to replace Abraham's son as a burnt offering. This same story appears in both the Qur'an and the Torah, but whereas Jews and Christians believe that Abraham was preparing to sacrifice Isaac (as mentioned in the Hebrew scriptures), Muslims believe it was Ishmael (the Qur'an does not mention the son's name). We had been wandering through the slum community—back when we were still searching for a room to rent—and we had stopped to have sweets at the house of a woman who had a room available. Suddenly two young girls—in a riot of purple tulle and sequins, decked out in dark sunglasses, headbands, hair clips, costume jewelry, and glitzy shoes—appeared and told us that their mother was calling us. We later learned that because they had not yet reached puberty, these girls were exempt from the requirements of modesty and seclusion indoors, so they were free to roam around the neighborhood as they pleased. We hadn't ever met their mother, but we were eager to make connections in the neighborhood, so we followed the girls back to their house, where we sat around on their *taakat*, chatting with Amna and her six daughters and chowing down on one of the most expensive meals they would prepare all year: goat curry.

Once we got to know Amna, we were surprised that she had been so welcoming of us from the very beginning, for we must have struck her as a mysterious pair of Angrez, or "Britishers," as all white foreigners are often called in India, who wandered into the neighborhood out of nowhere. Though she was a warm-hearted, loyal friend and a compassionate, calm mother, she was religiously conservative, with very traditional notions about how men and women should interact. Because her life had not been easy, and she had few dependable allies, she didn't open her heart or home to many people beyond her own blood relatives and trusted friends.

Her husband had gone missing nearly a year before—he had left for work one morning and never came home. She had gone to the police for help, but they had refused to look for him. His parents had also been oddly unhelpful in the search. When she asked his co-workers at the tailoring shop where he had been employed, they told her,

"What business is it of yours whether he came in to work or not?"

Hearing her story made me suspect that her husband had planned to disappear, perhaps in order to shake the responsibility of providing for a wife and seven children (six of them daughters, for whom he would have to scrape together dowries in the near future). Yet it was hard to imagine that he had made such a cold-blooded calculation when all of the children in the family seemed to have such warm, affectionate memories of their father. Yes, Amna confided, he had beaten her in the early years, and there had been trouble with her in-laws throughout the marriage, but in her opinion he was a good man: he didn't drink, he worked a steady job as a tailor, and he sewed clothes for the kids and brought home special treats for them at festival times.

If the possibility of his having intentionally abandoned the family had occurred to Amna or her children, they never mentioned it. He could have been killed by *goondas*, lawless thugs who sometimes mugged and brutalized people, or did dirty work on behalf of others. Or maybe he had been arrested and was being held indefinitely in some anonymous prison.

At any rate, with their sole breadwinner suddenly gone, the family was in dire straits. The only son, Shaqeel, was a skinny, serious teenager whose deep voice seemed disproportionately large for his slight frame. He had dropped out of high school to start a recycling shop that would help keep food on the table and pay the fees to keep his younger sisters in school. In the absence of his father, he was hoping to save up his earnings to pay for his sisters' dowries one at a time. Yet Julekha, the eldest daughter, had to delay her marriage indefinitely because Shaqeel could not manage to scrape together enough for a dowry. But the worst part of their situation was not knowing what had happened to their husband and father.

In spite of Amna's wariness of outsiders, she and her children opened their home, hearts, and lives to us. Eventually, she accepted us as her son and daughter-in-law, telling us repeatedly that her house was our house, and we could come over whenever we wanted. Sometimes, when Andy would drop by to pick up something from the store, Amna's family would run out of their back room and invite him in for tea, even if there was no other man at home. Because this would have been considered improper with men who weren't related by blood or marriage, it powerfully demonstrated their acceptance of us into their family.

Amna and her family named me Umera, which means "pure heart," so that I would have an Urdu name like my new sisters, as Amna's daughters came to consider themselves. Because my English name was difficult to pronounce, everyone in the neighborhood called me either Umera, or, among the kids, *Didi* or *Aapi*, which mean "older sister." Amna's family named Andy Gulzar, which means "Rose"—something I teased him about until I heard other men in the community respond to it with almost reverent approval. But the name that stuck was Andy *bhai*—"Andy brother"—a mark of familiarity that was used by everyone in the neighborhood, from small children to grey-bearded old men.

* * *

One day, I walked into the courtyard to bring in my clothes from the laundry line and found our landlady, Gita, sitting with Amna. Gita had dislocated her shoulder when she had fallen from the top of her stairs onto her son's motorcycle. For the next several days, she suffered such immense pain that she had to stop wearing her sari blouse because it hurt too much to move her shoulder in and out of the sleeve. Gita was sitting in the sun completely topless, crying with pain, while Amna sat across from her, covered head to toe in full *niqab*. I was struck by the ease of their inter-religious friendship as Amna, a strict and conservative Muslim, comforted Gita, who was Hindu. After we exchanged greetings, I saw Amna sweep her hand toward Gita's bosom and remark calmly, "Why don't you...cover this?"

Moments such as these made me realize that our neighbors' ability to coexist with people of different faiths was another manifestation of *jugaad*. In their hometown rural villages, our neighbors would have been surrounded by others who shared their religious beliefs. But here in the hodgepodge of the city, polytheistic vegetarians and monotheistic meat-eaters had learned to live side by side in relative peace—in spite of the history of bloodshed between them. Neighbors celebrated one another's religious festivals, and Hindu complaints about goat slaughtering and Muslim jokes about idol worship remained private and fairly good-natured. Their common national identity as Indians held them together in a fragile but significant alliance, prompting them to sometimes speak of each other as siblings who drove each other crazy but ultimately loved one another.

Because most of our friends in the slum were only vaguely aware of any religious identities other than Hindu and Muslim, they tried hard to categorize us as one of their own. Though we didn't pray *namaz* (the liturgical prayer offered by Muslims in Arabic five times a day) or perform *puja* (Hindu worship ceremonies), religion in India is not only about spiritual practice; it defines identity, family, and culture. We had shown up without an extended family, with no recognizable regional dialect or religious vocabulary, and we claimed to have no caste. Moreover, we were white foreigners, yet we didn't act like the *Angrez* they had seen on TV. Where was my bikini? Why weren't we living a lifestyle of "free sex" or eating the strange things that they had seen "our people" consume on *Man vs. Wild*?

Knowing the connotations of British colonial rule, wealth, and Western culture—everything from "love marriages" to jeans to MTV, not to mention the insensitive proselytism that typified many evangelicals—we usually avoided using the term "Christian" to describe ourselves. Many of our neighbors actually believed this term to be a marker of caste rather than belief, and the last thing we wanted was to be treated like some kind of wealthy patrons. We wanted people to see our lives and decide for themselves what kind of people we were, instead of putting us into the Christian box right away, tainted as it was with negative misconceptions.

When our neighbors asked us directly about our religious identity, we would say, "We are followers of Jesus, peace be upon Him." Some would immediately respond, "Oh, so you're a Muslim!" Because we wanted to operate under their understanding of religious categories—not our own—we would nod our heads.

Others would say, "Oh, so you're a Christian!" Again, we would nod our heads.

Some would ask. "Are you a Hindu?"

"We believe that there is only one God."

"Yes, there is only one God, God is one. So do you pray *namaz*?"

"No, but we pray *dua*." This meant freestyle prayer from the heart, another form that was familiar in Islam.

"Why don't you pray *namaz*?"

"Because in the same way that you follow Muhammad, we follow Jesus, and He gave us a different way to pray. We pray in the way that He taught us."

"Do you read the Qur'an?"

"No, but we read the *Injil*." The *Injil* is the Arabic name for the four canonical gospels, which are also considered holy books in Islam, albeit corrupted. Some people took pity on us for not knowing Arabic, and they would exhort us to read the Qur'an or would offer to teach us *namaz*.

As I developed a deeper relationship with Amna, we had many conversations about following Jesus and reading the gospels. Even though I neither fasted during *Ramazan* nor prayed *namaz*, whenever she introduced me to a relative or friend, she would always tell them that I was a Muslim. It was as though the term Muslim was simply her way of saying, "This is a good person. You can trust her."

* * *

One day, I accompanied Amna to the bank to open a new account. After we had finished all of the necessary paperwork, we started down the stairs to the ground level of the building. Casually, Amna approached a short gray-haired man with striped boxers and a rounded belly partially concealed under a grimy, white tank top. He looked homeless, but their interaction was so familiar that they seemed to know each other.

"So you're here every day?" I heard Amna ask, pointing to a padlocked closet that seemed strangely out of place underneath the stairs of the shopping complex.

On the way home, Amna explained to me that the pot-bellied man had spiritual power to discern information from objects, and she had given him a piece of her husband's clothing so that he could tell her where her husband was. I was surprised that my devout Muslim friend would turn to a Hindu psychic for answers, but the situation reminded me of just how desperate her circumstances were—and how interfaith *jugaad* manifested itself in India.

A few days after our trip to the bank, Amna asked me to accompany her to the psychic to give him another piece of her husband's clothing for divining purposes. "He lost the other cloth I gave him—it fell out of his pocket," she told me.

"How much does this service cost?" I asked as we crossed the bridge spanning the swirling, black sludge of the drainage canal that snaked alongside the slum.

"I don't know," she said. "I pay him after I get my answer."

Knowing that this was a last-ditch attempt at closure, I didn't want to discourage her too much, but I cautiously warned Amna that the man might just give her whatever answer he thought would bring him the most money.

She shrugged.

A few days afterward, I inquired about the result of the divination.

"He says he lost that second piece of cloth, too." Amna laughed soberly. "I decided to forget about it. He's no use."

Losing her husband in such a mysterious way had thrust Amna into the life of a widow, but without the closure of a funeral or the support that sympathetic in-laws or a government widow's pension might have provided. Amna saw this catastrophe as the source of all the hardship in her life. Before her husband's disappearance, she hadn't had to worry about finances—the family had not been wealthy, but they had been able to buy new clothes when they needed them, they had paid school fees on time every month, and they had never skipped a meal. Amna's husband had also been the one responsible for negotiating with the outside world: she depended on him to deal with bills, legal issues, house repairs, and everything else that lay beyond the domestic realm of cooking, cleaning, and raising children. "When you lose your husband," she lamented, "What's left?"

Yet I could see that with her husband gone, Amna had been given the chance to discover what was left. She was discovering her own capabilities as she traveled around the city by herself to take her children to the doctor, meet with school administrators, and open a bank account of her own. I was proud of my friend's strength and ingenuity in forging her independence and finding ways to care for her family in spite of the odds stacked against them. When I pointed this out, Amna seemed to take pride in her accomplishments—yet I also knew that she would have gladly exchanged her new "freedom" to return to the safety and familiarity of having a man in charge.

* * *

After adopting us as part of her family, Amna invited us to a cousin's wedding in her home village. Everyone in the village lived in large houses of extended families, sharing common life together. One of the family homes we visited housed around fifty people. In these extended households, the family acted as a supportive community, providing safety and security for everyone and sharing both economic and emotional burdens.

We knew Amna and her family were excited to introduce us to all of their relatives (which were legion), and we were glad to have an opportunity to demonstrate how much we valued our relationship with them. Yet we struggled with the round-the-clock social time (we were never alone) and also with being the constant center of attention and curiosity.

Because I had already attended several other Indian weddings, I knew that there would not be much of an event to witness because the *nika*—the signing of the marriage contract— typically happened behind closed doors. The main venue of the first wedding we had attended was the dirt path in front of the bride's house, along which hundreds of water buffalo came stampeding back and forth from their watering hole every few minutes. At one point, Andy nearly got stampeded when the buffalo came thundering along unexpectedly—and later, he had to whisk a stray toddler out of one's path. At another wedding in our neighborhood, a fight broke out when people who had not been invited to the wedding—but who lived in the row of shacks adjacent to the giant pink wedding tent—crashed the celebration and started to scarf down the free buffalo *biryani* and *jaarda* (sweetened orange rice). Needless to say, by the time we attended the village wedding, we knew—more or less—what to expect.

As with all Indian weddings, the guests were strictly segregated along gender lines. As Andy took his place among the men sitting in plastic chairs, I went upstairs to a tiny room, where a group of women and girls—all decked out in shiny, sequined clothes and heavy make-up— crowded around the bride, primping and preening as they prepared for the arrival of the groom.

I sat on the floor with the rest of the women, waiting for the moment that the groom would sign the wedding contract and the bride, like a decorative object, would be handed over from her father's possession into her husband's. This moment of farewell was not unlike a funeral, and it always made me sad. Though I never really knew what the bride or the other women were feeling at this moment, every bride I had seen had looked terrified and miserable.

When we heard the groom and all his friends and relatives arriving in a noisy procession with drums and dancing, the bride burst into tears. A group of serious-looking men in traditional religious garb entered the small room, and we squeezed against the walls to make room for them. The bride lowered her head and hid beneath the sweep of her shawl, clutching her aunt's hand.

The mullah sat down in the middle of the room with a book and read out the lines of a prayer in Arabic. Another man stood over the bride, stooping down to listen for her faint voice as she repeated the prayer. Then, following custom, the mullah asked her three times whether she chose to enter into marriage with the groom. The rest of the men stood as a cloud of witnesses at the door to attest to the fact that she had given her consent, but her small voice was barely audible, and I was sitting just a few feet away from her. Following each repetition of the question, the man standing over her strained to make out her timid agreement: "*Kubul kiya.*" Then she signed (or thumbprint-ed) the contract, and the men left. That was the *nika*, and with the completion of that ceremony, the couple's marriage had officially begun.

By the time the women had served the men dinner, eaten their own, and finished cleaning up after the day's festivities, it was nearly midnight. The strict separation between the genders at weddings always bothered me. I hated the way the men were always served first and how they held the role of actors—dancing, eating, and occupying public space—while the women were the passive observers.

When it was finally time for bed, I had to sleep shoulder-to-shoulder with six other women and girls, who were all related and had grown up with the habit of sharing small spaces, casually throwing arms and legs across each other in the night and snuggling up next to one other to find a comfortable position. This cultural cuddling made me claustrophobic. It was as if Indian society required me to be an extrovert even while sleeping. We slept with the lights on to humor one of the woman's babies, who purportedly was afraid of the dark and would cry if the lights went out. Yet even with the lights on, the baby was awake and crying much of the night. I awoke at dawn with a stranger's hand on my sternum, and when I rolled toward the wall to try to regain some personal space, the girl simply turned with me and moved into a spooning position. Not long afterward, I resigned myself to being awake and walked into the family courtyard with tired eyes, where I was greeted with a warm smile from Amna and the hospitable question, "Did you have a good rest?"

Andy spent the night on a wooden platform without a mattress, which he shared with the mullah who had officiated the ceremony. By the time he woke up the next morning, a third man was fast asleep between them.

After every wedding I ever attended in India, women always asked me, "Did you cry like this on your wedding day?" I was never sure how I should answer. Yes, I cried, I would think, but not like this. I wasn't leaving my family, old life, and whole world behind at the end of the night only to step into a new house, new family, new community, and new life with complete strangers, where I could anticipate hostility and abuse.

* * *

One afternoon, I returned to our neighborhood after spending the day in an office, where I volunteered with a women's rights organization, writing reports and translating case histories from Hindi into English. After reading an article in an English language newspaper about the public outrage over a local politician's recent announcement, made at a political rally, that any girl who had sex with a boy outside of marriage should be hanged, I had asked my Indian co-worker how a candidate who said such things could ever get re-elected. As a lawyer for a human rights organization, my co-worker had shared my disgust, observing that the politician had probably been trying to appeal to the rowdy men in the "backwards" outpost where the rally had been held.

On my way home, I passed Amna, who was sitting in her doorway tying strings onto eyeless cardboard faces, which were heaped in a pile beside her.

"Here, take one!" Amna said playfully, holding up one of the visors. I recognized the face of the politician I had read about in the newspaper.

"I'm hardly going to put one of those on," I joked back, "when he says that girls should be hanged for running away with their boyfriends."

The lighthearted tone fell from Amna's voice. "But that's exactly what should happen!"

I was taken aback. "And the boys?" I asked.

"They should both be hanged!" she replied emphatically.

We fell into a long, heated argument. Especially since I had never even seen her use physical discipline with her children—highly unusual in a community where parents frequently hit children in anger—I was incredulous that she would support such a violent law. She couldn't get past the seriousness of shaming one's family and breaking a parent's heart by running away and marrying a spouse of one's own choosing.

One of her daughters was standing nearby, a girl in her early teens. I took her hand. "If she ran away with her boyfriend—I know you don't really have a boyfriend, Rubi—then you would be angry and sad. But would it make you happier if she died?"

"Yes, it would," Amna replied firmly. "I would say to her, 'Stand up. Put the noose around your neck.'"

I shook my head. "I don't believe you. You don't really believe that!"

Amna dug in her heels. "If one daughter goes bad, then the next sister will see it and do the same, and the next, and the next." I knew that she was thinking of her six daughters.

"If the human heart is a glass of water," I said, "it contains neither completely pure nor completely dirty water, but there's a little of both. And if someone does something wrong—especially if a young person makes a mistake—

then there's a chance that even though she's wandered off the right path, she'll eventually come back. But if we kill her, there's no chance for her to change—no chance for God to change her heart." I put my hand on Amna's arm. "Do you really support a law that puts punishment ahead of mercy?"

Our animated conversation drew in a man who was standing in the alleyway outside the doorway. As the man listened, I told Amna the story of the prodigal son, explaining how the younger of two sons had shamelessly asked for his inheritance in advance without even waiting for his father to die, and how he had taken the money and ran away to a foreign country to squander it all on buying sex and throwing wild parties. I told her how the younger son had run out of cash and been forced to take the disgusting job of tending pigs (*harami!*), and how he had looked with longing at the scraps of food reserved for the filthy animals under his care. I explained how the starving son had realized that his father's servants were living better than he was—and though he knew he could never be accepted back into the family because he had dishonored his father, he could ask to be taken on as a lowly servant in the household. Then I told her how the young son returned to face his father, expecting punishment—but his father surprised him by running out to meet him, throwing his arms around him in loving welcome, and throwing a party to celebrate his homecoming.

"Jesus says that God is like the father in that story," I said. "Maybe He is angry when we run away, but He's more sad than angry, and He loves us so much that He's always hoping that we will come back someday."

Both Amna and the man from the alleyway were smiling now. *Yes, God is like that*, they seemed to be thinking.

But then Amna told me that it was different in India. She told me how she knew parents who had died of heart attacks and grief after their children had eloped. "What a terrible thing those couples did to their parents!"

I agreed that children should consider their parents' well-being, but I asked if parents should also consider the feelings of their children. "You're a mother," I said. "I've seen the way you're always putting your kids ahead of yourself. If there's not enough food, you feed them first. If you're tired but there's work to be done, then you do it."

She nodded.

"So why can't parents put their children's needs ahead of their own in marriage?"

"Maybe over there, you can choose who you want and make yourself happy, but here it's different."

I asked her to consider the young couple who lived down the street. The woman had married a kind and responsible husband who held a steady job and treated both her and their young daughter with gentleness and respect. But because they had a love marriage, the woman's parents had refused to speak to their daughter ever since the wedding—even though they lived directly across the street, just a few feet apart. They had tried to dissuade their daughter from the relationship by beating her and locking her up in the house. I asked why the girl's parents couldn't forgive their daughter, accept her choice, and welcome her back into the family so that they could continue to have a relationship with their child."

"No, they could never do that. It wouldn't be like it was before," Amna insisted. "That doesn't happen here."

***

When Amna's elderly aunty from a neighboring slum visited, Amna invited me to stop by her house so we could meet one another. Despite the oppressive heat of the room, Amna's eldest daughter, Julekha, served us steaming cups of tea as a gesture of hospitality as we sat on the sagging wooden boards of her *taakat*, polished smooth from years of use. That single piece of furniture served as dining table, sofa, kitchen counter, and bed in Amna's simple house.

Amna asked about my sister's pregnancy back in the States. "She says she's having trouble sitting up again after she lies down," I said, pantomiming the awkward weight of a big belly preventing me from sitting upright.

The women laughed.

"Of course, I don't know anything about that since I've never been pregnant," I continued, "but I'm sure that was a familiar experience for you."

Amna's face grew serious, almost offended. "No, that never happened to me," she declared. "I kept working and walking around until the moment I gave birth, so I never had that problem. Ask her," she said, motioning to her relative. "She gave birth to twelve children!"

The older aunt nodded with dignity. "It's the women who lie around resting too much who have trouble," she confirmed. "Their babies aren't born naturally. They're always the ones who have their babies by big operation. I never had any pain during pregnancy. Ask a doctor, and he'll tell you—don't lie around and rest too much."

"Yes, just keep walking around," Amna agreed. "That way the baby will come sooner."

They went on to describe how they had gone on lifting heavy buckets and squatting to wash dishes and scrub laundry by hand up until the moment that each of their children was born at home. After giving birth, they had always gone back to their routine of housework later the same day.

The previous year, I had accompanied another neighbor to the emergency room after heavy lifting had sent her into labor two months early, but I didn't bring this into the conversation.

"These days men are making girls so fragile," the aunty sighed.

"What do you mean?" I asked.

"Nowadays, girls just say, 'Oh, I have a headache,' or, 'I feel tired!'" she mocked. "And then their men say, 'You lie down, I'll cook,' or, 'Just rest while I take care of the baby.' You know what used to happen when we were young? The baby would cry and the man would just sit there and say, 'Your baby is crying.'"

"Also, girls do naughty things nowadays," Amna added. "They go from one boy to another all the time."

I tilted my head. "Are you saying that girls have become more fragile because they're promiscuous?"

"Yes, exactly," Amna replied.

But the aunty shook her head. She said that men were making women fragile by helping too much at home. "When we were young, we had to do all the housework, whether we felt sick or tired or not."

I suggested that perhaps the men were becoming less fragile than they had been in the past, since they had previously been incapable of feeding themselves or caring for children.

The aunty just shrugged, but it occurred to me that I had best tread carefully in that vein of thought. There was a narrow line between communicating the injustice of their suffering and taking away the identity the women had built around weathering this hardship well. They didn't see themselves as victims—perhaps not even as survivors—but as noble women who had endured necessary female suffering and faced the world alone, growing strong in their roles as wives and mothers.

I admired their strength and determination. And I knew that as widows, they would never experience partnership or respect from men during the remainder of their lives. So I didn't want to take away their source of pride and identity by reframing their struggle as an unnecessary consequence of men's laziness.

Yet I also knew that the patriarchal traditions of male power, female modesty, and the separation of women were not serving Amna and her family well. With only one teenage son and no grown man, they were often desperate for money, falling behind with expenses for medicine, school fees, and the debts Amna's husband had left behind when he disappeared. Living under such constant financial pressure, Amna had told me once that she had thought of drinking poison and giving it to all of her children at the same time in order to spare them all from a continued life of hardship.

In spite of her desperation, she refused to work as domestic help in another family's home, since she viewed it as immoral and unclean for a woman to work outside the home. And when Andy suggested a job for her oldest daughter at a nearby coffee shop, with a potential salary of 6,000 rupees a month, Amna replied, "How could Julekha work outside?" She couldn't have her teenage daughter working in public and interacting with men. And she found the idea of Julekha wearing a uniform—pants and a collared shirt in place of traditional Indian clothing—unthinkable and shameful.

Amna's traditional mindset often seemed to be the biggest obstacle when Andy and I tried to help her find solutions to the problems that she shared with us. Yet I also understood that it must have seemed impossible for her to criticize these customs, laws, and beliefs—even when they seemed to be working against her. For if she lost these aspects of her identity—which she had worked so hard to defend—perhaps she would feel that she had nothing left. Without that safety and security, the world as she knew it would no longer make sense.

* * *

Early one morning, I found Amna standing on the roof outside my door. The sadness in her eyes belied her stony expression as she told me that a relative's one-month-old son had died during the night. Her brow was furrowed, her voice quiet and matter-of-fact. "Eat breakfast and then come," she said.

I walked down the alleyway to the open space where the brick houses met the plastic shacks. In keeping with north Indian Muslim culture, someone had hung a white funeral tent over a *taakat*, where I could see the small, shrouded form of a baby. In Asia, white—rather than black—is the color of death.

The baby's mother knelt in front of the *taakat* on woven mats, her body shaking as she quietly cried. A handful of other women and children had gathered around her and would remain with her for most of the day—not so much to console her, but to bear witness to her grief and cry alongside her. When I sat down next to the mother, someone uncovered the baby's face for me to see. He was so small and so perfect that it really looked as if he might only be sleeping. As soon as she saw him, the mother began sobbing uncontrollably, crying out for her son again and again.

Other women gathered around me, explaining that the baby had had diarrhea the day before, and after giving him some medicine in the evening, the family had gone to sleep, thinking he would be fine. In the early hours of the morning, his mother had tried to feed him as usual, but he never woke up.

The suddenness of the whole thing shocked me. How many children in our neighborhood had suffered diarrhea at some point? Who would have thought that a perfectly healthy baby could be dead in a single day from something so commonplace? Up until then, I had been confused by my neighbors' apparent paranoia when it came to health, taking their kids to the doctor for every little cold and cough. But sitting next to the dead boy's mother, I understood that with every illness—no matter how minor—memories of other lost children reminded parents that this could be the fever, cold, or cough that suddenly ended their child's life, for reasons that they would never understand.

I knew that we would never know if that baby boy had died from dengue fever, or some other mosquito-borne illness, or from dehydration, or because his mother was anemic during pregnancy (which is the case for nearly three quarters of poor women in India). Most likely, his birth had not been officially registered, so his death would never be reflected in child mortality statistics. His mother had lost a child before—perhaps in similarly baffling circumstances. But even if his death had been preventable, I knew his mother would never be given information about how to prevent the deaths of other children in the future.

Later that same day, I was coming out of a friend's house when I found Amna standing on a corner where I'd never seen her before.

"What are you doing here?" I asked.

"Looking for you. A little boy on my street is dead. Come," she said.

Like the baby, this three-year-old boy had apparently been healthy up until the last moment. He had come down with a fever, had seemed to get better after taking medicine, and then was back out in the street playing as usual. But then he had died.

Again, I sat next to the mother under a white funeral tent, staring at the tiny, motionless body of a little boy who looked as if he might be sleeping. Stories about the circumstances surrounding the child's death passed from one person to another as neighboring mothers arrived, holding crying babies on their hips. Children ran up and down the alleyway on either side of the tent as the relatives of the young boy wept and wailed. As I sat next to Amna alongside the grieving mother, siblings, aunts, and grandmothers, I felt their sadness seep into me.

At first, I was uncomfortable with these noisy, crowded rituals, since North American culture tends to treat grief as a private affair with distance and silence. I was accustomed to the reverent hush of a funeral home and the solitary contemplation of a graveside service—not the emotional displays of an Indian funeral. But I came to value my neighbors' public mourning. Though they were all well-acquainted with grief, that didn't dull their pain. As they sat around the body together, they entered one another's sorrow through their own experiences of loss. The young grief-stricken mother knew that she was not alone, because everyone gathered around her had experienced what she was going through—and this freed her to express her pain and sorrow.

As I sat beside my Indian neighbors, I kept wondering what Jesus meant when He said: "Blessed are those who mourn . . . for they shall be comforted."[6] If God knows what it is like to lose a son, then God must also mourn. If God knows the grief of watching precious children die of preventable disease, violence, and poverty, then those who mourn must be connected with God's heart in an intimate way. Perhaps Jesus meant that those who mourn will be comforted when His Kingdom comes—when all things will be set right, when people, families, and societies will be restored, when life to the fullest will be the rule instead of the exception.

Yet as I looked at the face of the grieving mother sitting next to me, I wondered what words of comfort Jesus would have for her right then. I was struck by the fact that

---

[6] Matthew 5:4

this mother was blessed in that moment because of the way she was facing her loss, sharing her pain with others, and enduring—rather than denying or repressing—the process of mourning. She was blessed in that moment because through her mourning, she was receiving comfort from the community around her. In the midst of that noisy, weeping crowd, I realized how often I had missed out on the blessing that was meant to come in the midst of pain— because too often I had shoved my pain deep into my subconscious rather than freely and fully expressing it.

When a group of men came to wrap the body and carry it to the graveyard for burial, a wail rose from the crowd of mourning women. After this moment of final separation, the mother would never see her child's face again— for most families in the slum didn't have photos of their children.

For the second time that afternoon, Andy accompanied the group of men to the graveyard, helping to carry the small body, which felt much too light. Both times, he watched over the coffin while the other men went into the mosque to pray *namaz* on the way to the cemetery. Then he helped to bury each child as, one by one, the men poured handfuls of dirt into the grave.

* * *

Several months later, I sat with Amna on the stoop outside her house as she told me about her recent financial difficulties. The entire family had fallen ill at the same time, and the medical expenses had added up. A large Christian aid organization had recently provided her with the initial stock to start a small store in her back doorway, selling snacks and a few staples, such as lentils and flour—but so far, the small business wasn't making any difference in her financial situation. She said she was going to have to take change out of the little tin cashbox in her store to buy vegetables for dinner.

Just then, four staff members from the Christian aid organization—a female social worker and three men who worked in the project office—showed up at the back door. Everyone in our community addressed these officials as the Big Ma'am and the three Big Sirs. They said they were stopping by to see how things were going with the store. Amna straightened and parted the curtain that separated her front room from the shop in her back doorway. As she walked over to meet them, I stood with her teenage daughters behind the curtain, invisible from the outside, but able to see through the lightweight fabric. I watched Amna slip into presentation mode, stiff and formal.

"How are things going with the store?" the Big Sirs asked.

"Great," Amna said. "Before, we had problems with food, but now things are okay."

"Call the child," they said, meaning the youngest daughter, who was the sponsored child. Sufiya raced across the room from where she had been standing with us behind the curtain, and Julekha began frantically trying to comb down her hair, put in a clip, and make her presentable. Amna called Sufiya again, sounding irritated. It wasn't that the visitors were showing any signs of being demanding or impatient, but Amna seemed to know that because they were the patrons, she must meet their expectations.

Amna called out again, and Julekha gave up trying to put in the hair clip. Sufiya ran to the back door to stand next to Amna. One of the Big Sirs took out his camera to take a photo of Amna and Sufiya standing in front of the shop. I knew the aid organization had donated the initial stock, and I figured the caption beneath the photo would mention that they were "providing this family with a much-needed livelihood" in the letter they would send to the sponsor, who was undoubtedly living somewhere far away.

"Smile!" the man said.

Then they left, and Amna returned to the front room, where we were still waiting behind the curtain. She sat down and sighed.

"You said you were hardly making any profit from this store. You still don't have enough money for food or medicine. Why didn't you tell them the truth?"

"*Unse kyaa matlab hai*?—What do they care?" she said. The visitors from the aid organization didn't seem to be interested in knowing what she thought—and she figured that nothing she said would make a difference.

Just then, a customer arrived. Amna pulled out the box where chewing tobacco was hidden away and handed a couple of packets to the man at her door. Though the aid organization had forbidden her to sell those products in her store, they were the only thing that turned a profit. The colored packages of cookies, candy, and salty snacks didn't make her any money.

"The things they gave me don't sell," Amna said. "They should have just given me money, and I would have bought things for the store myself."

I found myself wondering if that would have made much difference, with all the similar little doorway shops in our neighborhood. Surely there was not enough demand to warrant the supply. Moreover, none of the shop owners could read or write, and they had no knowledge of accounting.

The photo of Amna and her daughter made me angry, because I knew it was a lie. Amna's family was still constantly worried about how to stay afloat financially, and they were still going into debt over basic healthcare and school fees. When I had sponsored a child as a college student, I had assumed that the smiling face looking back at me from the photo on my fridge was out of danger now that a big aid organization had intervened. There in the slum, I was seeing the less-than-satisfying reality up close. I understood the marketing of the whole thing, and how an organization could raise more money by turning compassion into a canned, feel-good experience that could be personalized to appeal to consumers. Just thirty dollars a month to change somebody's life forever—what a good deal. But I knew first-hand that such bargains didn't exist in the real world.

Though I believed it was important to build relationships with marginalized people instead of just throwing money at them, I didn't have compelling charts and numbers to prove the effectiveness of my friendships in terms of development. Though I had known Amna and her family for almost two years—and we'd shared stories and time and had a deep sense of connection—our relationship hadn't made a measurable impact on their finances. The stresses in their life were essentially the same as when Andy and I had first met them. But they were honest about those problems. Amna had cried, laughed, gotten angry, and argued with me—something she never would have done with a patron, boss, donor, or anyone she needed to impress to keep the relationship intact. And that trust went both ways. Amna had a key to our room so that her family could look after things whenever we were out of the country. When I had surgery to remove my gallbladder, Amna brought us meals during my recovery. And because Amna had accepted Andy into the family as her son, the social conventions that separated men from women no longer applied, and he was free to drink tea in their house even when she and her teenage daughters were the only ones home.

I knew I didn't have a cunning alternative to offer the aid groups. But I could say that after all the time spent cultivating friendship by taking Amna's kids to pick up report cards at school, helping out with English homework, or paying for the ingredients to share a holiday meal together, Amna and her family felt less alone in the world.

By living in such close proximity to others and with fewer barriers to hide behind, Andy and I had learned the discipline of vulnerability, which had enabled us to receive hospitality and help from our neighbors. We had also learned the discipline of humility as we realized that we often received more from others than we had to offer them. But our transparency with our neighbors only went so far: we struggled to communicate the difficult aspects of sharing life together. Sacrificing so much of our privacy in order to be available to others was often a strain, but in an effort to appear as dependable and helpful as possible, I was likely to mask my stress or tiredness under a smile and a nod when I should have been more honest about my limitations.

One day, an elderly local shop owner praised me for how respectable I looked in my modest Indian clothes and head covering as I stood in line to buy eggs. "She comes from a country where women walk around naked!" he said to the other customers. Everyone nodded their heads in approval.

Though I was uncomfortable with the idea of everyone assuming I was some kind of reformed Jezebel, I appreciated the compliment as it demonstrated how well we had integrated into the community. After I got home, Andy and I laughed about the man's outrageous perceptions of America, but I felt a tinge of pride about our cultural sensitivity.

Yet even though we knew that our neighbors took great pride in claiming us as their own, announcing that we spoke Hindi "just like them," we also longed for tangible results to prove the effectiveness of our relational approach. We wanted to see concrete improvements in our neighbors' lives.

* * *

One morning, I woke at three a.m. to the sound of people yelling outside. My foggy mind slowly processed the sounds—argument between neighbors? Domestic dispute? In the midst of all the shouting, I thought I could hear a boy screaming. *They must have caught the thieves*, I thought as I struggled out of bed. For the past two weeks, there had been a string of robberies in our slum, and it sounded as if our neighbors' pent-up fear and anger were now being unleashed.

I woke up Andy, and we got dressed and walked down to the public square at the end of our alley, where an angry crowd had gathered around a thirteen- or fourteen-year-old boy. Several men, who were known as alcoholics and wife-beaters in the neighborhood, were clutching the boy's shirt and shaking him as they yelled insults and twisted his arms. Amna, who was standing at the edge of the crowd, explained that one of her neighbors had caught the boy breaking into his house, and she had woken up when the boy ran across the plastic half-roof over her bed in an attempt to escape. She told me of the terror she felt as she heard his footfalls moments before he was captured by other neighbors who had heard the commotion.

I knew from previous conversations that Amna had lost several nights of sleep as she lay awake worrying that her store might be robbed of its meager merchandise, or her teenage daughters might be raped by the thieves prowling around the community. The string of robberies was a symbol of all the hardship and uncertainty in her life, and along with the rest of the crowd, she wanted the boy to be interrogated and punished.

Though the boy was certainly in distress, we didn't know what to do. If we called the children's aid organization we knew about, the staff's presence might stir up wrath from the community. Just the day before, a woman in the community had experienced an allergic reaction to "bad medicine" she had received during a free health exam, which the same organization had sponsored to promote awareness of their services. But if we called the police, we knew from past experience that they might only escalate the violence.

When one of the men in the crowd began to hit the boy, and one of the bigger, brawnier men lunged toward the boy and kicked him, Andy and I waded through the crowd, yelling, "Don't hit him! He's just a kid!"

Suddenly, everyone turned away from the boy and told us to go home.

"He's a thief!" one woman shouted. "You don't understand this because your paycheck comes from your relatives in America. We have to work hard for our money!"

This criticism was fair, but it was cutting to hear, since it sidelined us as outsiders who should mind our own business.

"I know he stole things—and that's wrong," I said calmly. "But what you're doing to him right now isn't any better."

"If you want to take responsibility for him, fine! You pay us back the money that we lost!" another woman yelled.

"Why don't you call the police?" Andy asked.

The crowd erupted in laughter. "The police won't do anything!" One man jeered, "They'll just let him go!"

"We know he had other adults with him," a woman explained. "We want him tell us who was with him."

Andy put his hand on the boy's shoulder and asked his name. "Little brother, all of these people are very angry with you. If you've stolen from them, you need to tell them right now. You need to tell them everything you know, or they're going to beat you."

"I have told them!" said the boy. "They don't believe me!"

"He's lying," one man shouted. "He said he doesn't have any parents and he's from the village."

Andy suggested talking to the boy in a more private place. "He's afraid with everyone out here yelling at him."

But the crowd was convinced that they could only get the boy to talk with threats and torture. A group of men broke away from the crowd and dragged the boy down the street. When we tried to follow them, a woman bear-hugged me from behind, while our neighbors demanded that we go home. Even Amna was supportive of the crowd's behavior. She insisted that the men were taking the boy back to his parents and seemed convinced that no one would really hurt him.

In spite of the crowd's resistance to our presence, Andy managed to follow the group of men and teenage boys. After several minutes, he came rushing back to tell me that the men had stripped the boy naked, tied him to a pole, and were burning him with cigarettes.

Amna stared at Andy. "No they aren't," she countered.

"I saw it myself," Andy insisted.

Amna fell silent, as if she were afraid to voice any dissent.

I shivered in my thin night dress, even though I had wrapped a thick wool shawl over my shoulders before leaving our home. As Andy and I walked back toward the small crowd, no one tried to stop us. The boy, who was completely naked, was tied to the pole, his hands bound over his shoulders. In spite of the torment, he refused to confess the names of the other robbers. Perhaps he knew that a confession to the taunting crowd might lead to his death at the hands of those he was protecting. Perhaps other adults had been forcing the boy to climb into houses at night to steal for them, and they had also threatened and intimidated him.

"Look," one of the men said as we approached, "he hasn't even shed a single tear!"

When Andy saw a friend in the crowd, he drew him aside to persuade him that the treatment was both excessive and futile. In time, the crowd began to urge the men to return the boy's clothes. Once he was dressed, the men led the boy back to the square, where several men from the crowd slapped him and threatened him with sticks and belts.

Then someone from the crowd cried, "Don't hit him!" And when a man lunged forward to kick the boy as he huddled on a doorstep against a wall, a woman stepped forward to shield him. As a teenager rushed toward the boy with a big stick, a man pushed him away. But when an elderly and frail man began to criticize the crowd for their treatment of the boy, the group laughed and roughly shoved him away.

I felt helpless and numb, rattled by the indifferent laughter of the women and girls standing next to me. Figuring that any further efforts to calm down the crowd might make things worse for the boy, Andy and I stood off to the side, monitoring the situation, but feeling powerless.

A few minutes later, we heard that someone had finally called the police, and we made our way home. We didn't want to be on the scene when they arrived, because we didn't want to be asked questions that might incriminate our neighbors. We knew there was no use in sending anyone to jail, since it would only drive more families into the desperate condition of being husbandless and fatherless.

From our perch on the rooftop, we watched and prayed over the square as the police arrived and took the boy into custody. We hoped he would be taken to a place of greater safety, but we knew that his arrest would most likely be another chapter in a long and painful ordeal with the government's Child Welfare Committee.

We felt somewhat nervous about how people would respond to us over the next few days, but we hoped that calmer conversations with friends would be more fruitful than the arguments we'd had in the pre-dawn hours of the morning. Even though we were disturbed by our neighbors' treatment of the boy, we didn't want them to think we were taking sides against them. We empathized with their fear, and we knew that our neighbors' poverty made them especially vulnerable to thieves, since they didn't have the means to protect the little they had. And without access to bank accounts, most people stored their life's savings inside their homes. Moreover, many of our neighbors' shacks didn't have doors, and the ladders that led up their rooftops provided easy access to thieves. Since the homes were packed close together, if a thief found his way into one home, he often had access to several at once. People who had so little were hit hard by the theft of a cell phone, a small stash of cash, or the merchandise for their small doorway stores.

We also knew that we had a much lower tolerance for violence than our neighbors did, since nearly all of them had been beaten as children (if not as adults), and so many of them beat their own children. From their perspective, perhaps some of the people in the crowd weren't doing anything to the thief that they wouldn't have done to their own kids. Where we perceived their actions as unjust, they must have viewed our interference as hypersensitive and nonsensical.

Because our friends had been actively involved in and supportive of the violence—or had laughed about it from a distance, mocking us for taking it seriously—Andy and I felt sad, confused, and alone. As we prepared for the day after our night of little sleep, I continued to be haunted and horrified by the animalistic, violent core that had been revealed in our neighbors. *So this is who they really are*, I kept thinking. *This is how they treat the people who get on their bad side*.

The next day, we learned from our neighbors that the police had demanded a bribe from Amna's neighbor, who had caught the boy breaking into his house. When her neighbor refused to pay, the police released the boy from the station without filing a report—or referring him to the Child Welfare Committee. Rather than protecting a vulnerable child from a dangerous situation and a vulnerable community from crime, the police had looked for a way to make easy money. With no higher authority to appeal to for help, we understood why our neighbors had wanted to take the law into their own hands.

"Next time we catch the thief, we're going to kill him with electricity," Amna told me defiantly when I saw her later that morning. I felt a shiver spread through my body as I pictured the mob taking one of the live wires hooked loosely into the power lines and walking toward the helpless boy, tied to a pole.

Amna was angry with me, and she felt that the police's corruption proved that the mob had been right. Though I shared Amna's anger toward the police, I argued that torture and interrogation had not drawn any information from the boy—much less returned any of the things that had been stolen. As we raised our voices at one another other, each unwilling to change our position, I didn't feel angry so much as hurt and alone, sad and disappointed.

As I left Amna's home and walked through our slum, I felt as if a big wall of ice had risen between us and our neighbors. *How can I continue living with them, joking and making small talk, with this huge rift between us?* I wondered. *How can I be authentic and honest when my actions only confuse and offend them?* I wanted to tell them that I was for them—that I empathized with their loss, anger, and frustration—but I was against their mob violence. Yet my neighbors didn't seem to be able to understand this distinction.

As I moved through the slum that I had come to see as our home, I realized that I could not simply project the evil onto "them." The violence was not unique to this particular group of people, but was embedded deep in the human heart—a terrifying possibility that we each contain. I knew it had been unleashed in my neighbors because their experience of the world had been largely violent and uncaring. When everything else was totally beyond their control, they had grasped after whatever power they could exert—scapegoating their anger onto the young boy.

I also knew that police and military within our own country continue to use similar tactics of interrogation and torture. In our developed and Christianized West, we continue to attack people and ideas that make us afraid. We continue to satisfy our lust for revenge through due process, relying on the impersonal systems of the state to carry out the bloodshed for us so that we can remain upright, law-abiding citizens.

As I walked through our slum that afternoon, everyone seemed to be carrying on with life as usual. People prepared for an upcoming festival, beating drums and hanging up decorations. In the same square where the boy had been tied to a pole and interrogated the night before, they held a religious gathering with prayer and scripture reading. Celebrations and tragedy flowed forward, side by side, unaffected by all our efforts. I wondered if our presence in the community had made—or would ever make—any difference.

I thought of the loan sharks, politicians, and police who came into our community wearing their indifference and contempt on their sleeves. I thought of the social workers and other "helpers" who strolled through our community, revealing their disdain through pity and condescension. I thought of the people who lived in the slum, who knew that they couldn't trust doctors, charities, government officials, or police—and so they resisted change, stuck to what they knew, and depended on one other.

Because we had white faces and foreign passports and Hindi was not our first language, we could never dissolve into our neighbors' society. But we had hoped this difference would be part of the gift that we would bring to our community. We asked questions and offered alternative ideas; we tried to help our neighbors see their lives and their world from a new angle and creatively respond to their circumstances. I remembered several occasions when we had validated a woman's feelings, questioned the harsh treatment of a child, and affirmed people in their skills and contributions to the community.

We also knew that our foreign identities had inherent power and cultural biases—and if we were going to catalyze change, we would have to become very different outsiders than our neighbors had encountered before. So we had tried to listen to our neighbors and humbly learn from the people who had been in the community for a long time. And we had hoped that we would be around long enough to become quasi-insiders ourselves.

Though we had known this process would take time, and our acceptance would never be as straightforward as if we had been born into the community, we had imagined slipping seamlessly into life there, almost becoming Indian ourselves. But our experience with the young thief had revealed the wide chasm that still separated us from our neighbors. As I returned to our tiny home in the slum, I realized that we would never be able to cross that chasm.

* * *

I became acutely aware of our inability to cross this divide whenever we cooked meals, because although we were surrounded by hunger and poverty in the slum, those things did not characterize our own experience. Andy and I cooked our meals based on our tastes, not whether we had enough cash on hand. If the price of onions or tomatoes skyrocketed, we might choose not to buy them as an act of solidarity with our neighbors—or because we wanted to avoid the embarrassment of having our neighbors witness our decadence—but never out of economic necessity.

We experienced this embarrassment first-hand when we made stir-fried okra for dinner after the price of okra had risen beyond our neighbor's daily wages—though we hardly noticed the change in price. The next day, Amna said bluntly, "Yesterday I saw Andy *bhai* coming back from the *bazaar* with okra. He didn't see me, but I saw him. Okra was forty rupees per kilo yesterday." That was about eighty cents at the time.

I shrank under her steady gaze, unsure of what to say. I understood that she wasn't angry, and that she was only trying to help us understand the difficulties and frustrations in her life, which we might not notice unless she brought them to our attention. But her comment made me feel guilty and uncomfortable. And I realized that clean, theoretical solidarity was much simpler than the day-to-day reality of a hundred little choices, habits, and perspectives that separated our experience from that of our neighbors.

For in spite of our deep friendship and the many ways that Amna had blurred the social and cultural lines that should have separated us, she was always aware of the distance between us. She knew that we were rich and she was poor. She knew that someday we would leave, and she had nowhere else to go. Yet Amna viewed our relationship through the lens of Indian family, in which nothing was too much to ask and interdependency was assumed—and this sometimes caused unspoken hurt and disappointment.

For living next door to hungry people, there was always the pressing and difficult question about how to love our neighbors genuinely when they were hungry and we were fed. As I came to care about Amna's daughters, I began to wonder why her teenage girls didn't have the opportunity to pursue their dreams of romance and adventure, which were not very different from my dreams at their age. And as I came to know Amna and other mothers, who—like my mother—wanted their children to be safe and happy, I had to consider why it was so much harder for these parents to provide a good life for their children. Because deep down, we were so similar.

Even as Andy and I came to realize that we would never be able to bridge the gap between our two worlds, it began to dawn on us that there are not two worlds, after all. There is no "ours" and "theirs." There is only one world, and we all share a common economy, a common ecology, a common humanity. Within this interdependent existence, Martin Luther King, Jr.'s words sound less political and ideological and more obvious and unavoidable: "Injustice anywhere is a threat to justice everywhere."

If our poorer neighbors in the developing world are suffering from the effects of depleted natural resources, polluted air, and poisoned water, then these problems will eventually ripple into the developed world—in spite of the layers of wealth and privilege that insulate us from one another. With every choice we make, we help to create— or destroy—the world that we share. My friendship with Amna, along with many others, drove me to examine the myriad ways that I was caught in this spider web of unjust relationships.

7
UNCOVERING THE FACE OF GOD

Fall 2013

"All will be well, and every kind of thing will be well."

—Julian of Norwich

As Andy and I began to sense that our small corner of the world was giving us a skewed view of the whole, we decided to retreat to the mountains for a few days so that we could continue to cope emotionally amidst the intense relationships and our ongoing encounters with illness, abuse, hunger, sickness, loss, and despair.

When we arrived at the remote ashram in the forest, we were overwhelmed by the natural beauty and silence around us. The gentle music of the birds and insects reminded us of life's original soundtrack—one that we had nearly forgotten amidst the mechanical roar of city life. We sat through a rainstorm, marveling at the genius of evaporation and clouds condensing and then bursting to nourish acre upon acre of trees. I cried as I encountered the goodness of God in the water falling in sheets over the unspoiled wilderness and the emerald lakes in the valleys below. At night, we stared with awe at countless stars in the sky, which we hadn't seen for months since they had been obscured by city lights.

Though I knew God was present in the city and the slums, I was often challenged to recognize Her presence within my fellow human beings. It seemed far easier to know God's gentleness and goodness when I was surrounded by the beauty of creation rather than human civilization. I thought of the trash-clogged, black, sludgy waterways, the polluted air, and the dismal lack of color in the many big cities I had visited throughout the world. For the moment, that all felt very far away. Feeling the peace of the mountains, I recognized how our alienation from nature in the city had eroded my sense of God's goodness.

* * *

The first day that we returned to our room in the slum, as I listened to the whir of the fan, the traffic horns, and the wail of a toddler in the alley downstairs, I realized that we were living a kind of fast—from stars, from external silence, from natural beauty. But I had to stop myself there, because I knew that there *was* beauty and goodness in the slums, though it was hard to recognize amidst the ugliness of poverty and violence—the trash strewn everywhere, the poor patients at the hospital who had to lie in their own blood for hours before any doctor or nurse paid attention, the children who were left crying alone in the street with no one to comfort them. Mother Teresa calls poverty Jesus' most distressing disguise, because in that filth, noise, and desperation, we often fail to recognize Him.

But I knew that God's goodness was there in the generosity of our landlady, bringing us some of the hot meal she had just prepared for her family because she wanted us to share the experience of a traditional food we had never eaten before. I saw joy in the smiles of our youngest neighbors. I saw mercy in the love that young mothers demonstrated by responding to the feeble cries of their helpless newborn babies. And I experienced grace when God carried me through days of anger, stress, exhaustion, or sadness through the support of my husband and friends.

Sometimes it takes a different kind of eye to recognize God With Us in the places where human brokenness has taken its toll, but when we find Her there, we have found God in the place She most desires to dwell with us.

I wanted eyes to see that beauty. I wanted the will to create more of it, to bring it to greater fullness. I wanted to uproot the weeds of injustice and fear that obscure God's goodness in the same way that city lights obscure the stars that are still present in the sky. When I thought of God's beauty in that way, then planting a garden, cleaning up trash, sharing a meal, or working to reconcile people to one another all seemed like part of the same thing: uncovering the face of God.

8

ZAHERA

Fall 2013–Spring 2014

"The way in which a faith community shapes language about God implicitly represents what it takes to be the highest good, the profoundest truth, the most appealing beauty...While officially it is rightly and consistently said that God is spirit and so beyond identification with either male or female sex, yet the daily language of preaching, worship, catechesis, and instruction conveys a different message: God is male, or at least more like a man than a woman, or at least more fittingly addressed as male than as female."

—Elizabeth A. Johnson

One day, a Christian social worker who was visiting me in the slum jubilantly assured me that God would protect me from suffering any of the parasitic illness that my neighbors endured from drinking dirty water, because God's favor rests on "His children" and "those who are doing His work." Feeling indignant about this picture that identified us as God's favorites while excluding others—particularly the many innocent children I knew—I told her that I didn't expect to be spared from the realities of living with the poor. In fact, I wondered if God might actually want us to share the suffering of others instead of avoiding their pain. This had certainly been my experience, for during my time in India, I contracted several rounds of amoebic dysentery, E. Coli, various bacterial infections, scalp fungus, and other strange conditions. Unpleasant, yes—but such things seemed to come with the territory of throwing in my lot with the poor. Because wasn't this the message of the incarnation? Hadn't God taken on human skin—and its myriad experiences of suffering—to reach out to humanity with love and compassion?

My friendship with Zahera, a spunky sixteen-year-old girl who lived on our alley, led me to think more deeply about how we are called to take on the responsibility for becoming the answer to one another's prayers. Every time I passed Zahera's doorway on my way to the local shop to buy rice or flour, she struck up a conversation with me. She was without a doubt the fastest-talking person I had met—and when I first met her, I stressed about being able to understand what she was saying. But within several months, I had Zahera to thank for my comprehension of rapid-fire, teenage girl Hindi, and I found myself rushing the pace of my speech to keep up with her exuberant staccato.

Zahera rarely ventured beyond her family courtyard or the nearby doorways of her friends, except to attend classes at a Muslim girls' school. Her father was dead; her mother had suffered for years from a debilitating illness that affected her mind as well as her body, and her older sister had a mental disability that prevented her from functioning beyond the level of a ten-year-old. Though her older brother worked, he had emotionally disengaged from the family and often gambled away his earnings on cricket games rather than bringing home money for food. This left Zahera as the primary caretaker of her mother and sister, and the one responsible for all of the cooking, cleaning, and laundry.

Zahera was highly intelligent, extroverted, energetic, and interested in everything, but the circumstances of her life offered her no opportunities to explore her own potential or the world beyond her muddy courtyard. She was imprisoned by poverty, unsympathetic male relatives, and the cultural attitudes that controlled and determined the course of her life. We both recognized the gulf between our experiences: I had traveled the globe, fallen in love, married the man of my choice, and made all of the decisions that had shaped the trajectory of my life. These were Zahera's dreams, too, but she was stifled, and I was powerless to free her.

* * *

One day, I visited Zahera and found her sitting in the family courtyard with her youngest aunt, who was also a teenager. Zahera had been dealing with cramps all day and complained out loud, "Ah, why do we have to have this filth every month?"

I laughed. "If it weren't for that filth, there wouldn't be any children, either!"

Zahera leaned forward in her chair and cocked her head to the side with interest. "What do you mean?" she asked.

"Do you know what causes the bleeding?"

She shook her head.

"Well, inside your womb, your body is building a nest for a baby," I began to explain.

I felt a bit silly about the whole nest metaphor, but it was the most straightforward way I could think to explain it—especially since I lacked precise medical vocabulary in

Hindi and was certain that a girl who had never learned about the purpose of menstruation wouldn't understand that vocabulary anyway.

"Every month, if you don't get pregnant, then your body cleans out that nest and starts building a new one," I continued. "The blood that comes out of your body is the stuff the nest was made out of. That's why pregnant women don't menstruate."

Zahera and her aunt stared at me in wide-eyed shock, their mouths hanging open. Slowly, the beautiful mystery of it all began to sink in, and Zahera smiled in wonderment. "I never knew," she said.

* * *

As Zahera's mother's condition rapidly deteriorated, Zahera began to take her mother on pilgrimages to a *mazar,* or Muslim saint's gravesite. Many of the sainted *baba*s were renowned for the supernatural powers they had exhibited during their lives, and they continued to be objects of devotion after their deaths. The numerous village *mazars* attracted religious pilgrims from across India—Muslim and Hindu alike—who came seeking miraculous healing or communion with God. In the absence of a medical solution, these pilgrimages helped Zahera cope with the mysterious wasting disease that caused her mother to hear voices and see people who weren't there, fearing that Satan inhabited their house and was going to kill her. With each episode of psychosis or increase in chronic pain, Zahera would seek refuge with her mother at the *mazar* and pray for protection and healing.

During a break between these pilgrimages, which became more and more frequent as time went on, I walked past Zahera's doorway and found her in a state of panic. She frantically asked us to help her look for her mother, who had slipped out of the house before breakfast and had been missing all day. Late that afternoon, we found her lying flat on her back in the dirt behind a local mosque near a symbolic tomb for Muhammad's grandson, Hussein. Zahera's mother alternated between talking in third person about killing a little girl and explaining wildly that she had left the house to escape Satan, whom a Muslim saint had told her was sure to kill her if she remained in the house. The sight of this feeble woman rolling around on top of these "graves" with matted, leaf-strewn hair, muttering about murder and Satan, sent shivers up my spine.

As Zahera watched her mother roll around on the ground, she sobbed hysterically—no doubt overwhelmed by worry, sorrow, and humiliation—while Andy and I tried to persuade her mother to come home. We prayed for her and tried to get her to sit up and drink water out of a bottle, as we figured she hadn't eaten or drunk anything all day. When nothing seemed to change, we called Zahera's older brother, who was out betting on a neighborhood cricket game with other teenage boys. Though he assured us he was on his way, long before he showed up, a man who lived across the alley from Zahera's family arrived on a motorcycle. He took the water bottle from us, recited a prayer in Arabic over the water and blew on it to bless it before giving it to Zahera's mother to drink. After drinking the water, she grew noticeably calmer. Andy and I stood to the side and watched in wonder as the neighbor's prayers seemed to subdue the demon within her.

"Won't you come home with us now?" the man asked her good-naturedly.

"Yes," she answered, "But only after *magrib ki azan*, the fourth call to prayer. I want to stay near Hussein until then."

"Okay," the man replied, nodding his head agreeably as if he were playing a make-believe game with a child. Then he looked up, as if listening for the call to prayer. After a few seconds of silence, he stood. "Alright, there it was. Time to go!"

Andy and I watched his wise and sensitive interaction in amazement. Typically, our neighbors—and men in particular—were not gentle or patient with people who were mentally ill or disabled. We were also confused about whether it was simply his respectful manner and his long history with Zahera's mother that had temporarily restored her to her senses, or whether his prayers and holy water had worked on a spiritual level to address the unseen power behind her suffering. We were intrigued to know what had made his prayers effective when our own prayers seemed to have made no difference. Once again, we were reminded of how little we knew about the mysterious ways that God worked in the world.

More and more, it seemed that the only thing we knew about prayer was what we didn't know. After I had prayed for a baby with diarrhea, her mother credited my prayers with the child's speedy recovery. And on another occasion, I prayed for a young Hindu girl on our street, whose migraine subsided when I pressed my hand to her forehead. But these experiences were rare and confusing in themselves. *Why bother?* I wondered when the baby who was healed got diarrhea again a few days later from living in the same filthy conditions that had caused the first bout. Why would God supernaturally intervene to cure diarrhea instead of intervening in the wider circumstances that left this child so vulnerable to disease in the first place? And why would God answer a fairly minor request to end a migraine, but remain silent to our plea for Zahera's mother to be healed from the terminal illness that held her entire family's life in limbo, preventing her daughters from attending school or sometimes being able to eat?

* * *

As Zahera's mother's condition continued to deteriorate without the hope of a cure, a new school year began and Zahera dejectedly confided in me that she would not be able to enroll because her family could not afford to pay for her textbooks and her mother's medications at the same time. I couldn't bear the idea of Zahera abandoning her studies, and I offered to accompany her to the market and buy the books myself.

Zahera's face lit up. "Really, Eshweety?" she asked, using her endearingly stylized pronunciation of my English name.

"Of course," I replied. "Education is important!"

"Oh, thank you, thank you, thank you, Eshweety!" she gushed, giving me a big hug.

Textbooks in hand, Zahera enthusiastically began classes, but she was forced to drop out of the local Muslim high school just a few months later. By then, her mother was in such poor health that Zahera needed to care for her full-time. Whenever I saw Zahera during this time, she poured out her sadness and frustration about abandoning her studies to tend tedious and endless household chores as she waited anxiously for her family to arrange her marriage.

Around this time, she heard about a Catholic nun who was offering a six-month tailoring course for teenage girls from the surrounding slums. The convent school was only a few minutes' walk away, and since classes were only held for two to three hours each day, Zahera could finish most of her housework and cooking ahead of time and leave her mother in her sister's care for the short time she was away. For Zahera and many others in our slum community (including Amna's daughter, Julekha), this class became virtually the only opportunity they had to leave the house—much less the neighborhood. The daily walk to class was also their only chance to escape household duties, hang out with friends, and act like the carefree teenagers they might have been in another life. Whenever Zahera described the afternoons she spent at the convent, her eyes lit up, and her voice filled with pride as she told me about the skills she was learning.

She also raved about the nun who ran the class. "I've told the Sister all about you!" she enthused. "She really wants to meet you! You should come to class with me someday. It's so much fun!"

Several hours hanging out with giddy teenage girls from all over the area who would be star-struck by the exotic American in their midst did *not* sound fun. It sounded like the classic "look-at-the-monkey-who-can-speak-Hindi!" situation, but I was intrigued to meet the octogenarian nun that Zahera and her friends so openly adored.

As we approached the convent, I was amazed to see dozens of Hindu and Muslim teenage girls from the slum, many wearing *niqabs* and veiling their faces, gathering enthusiastically around a wizened South Indian nun in her eighties. Each girl greeted Sister Veronica with deep respect and affection, and she mirrored their respect and love with her crinkly smile.

To begin class, the girls chanted a beautiful prayer together in Hindu style, yet with simple words that could be authentically prayed by a monotheistic Christian or Muslim as well.

After the class had settled into their work for the day, Sister Veronica led me outside to a chair under a gently swaying canopy of *neem* leaves to talk. Neither English nor Hindi was her mother tongue, and so I had a hard time deciphering her accent. Old age had also garbled her voice, which scraped slowly and painfully from her throat. Yet it was clear that she had a sharp mind and a lifetime's accumulation of wisdom. I had the impression that even her occasional long pauses and not quite on-topic comments were nuggets of wisdom—or Zen koans—that were going over my head.

She seemed to understand that these girls had precious little opportunity just to be kids, since most of them had been confronted with the realities of hunger, violence, and hardship from a young age—and long before their twentieth birthday, many would already be married off to complete strangers and pregnant, perhaps already caring for a baby or two. Without education or marketable experience, each of them would be completely dependent on her husband, whoever he turned out to be. Sister Veronica explained that the tailoring program might give some of the girls a means to earn a living, but more importantly, she hoped the course would instill a sense of confidence and self-worth in the girls while providing them a safe space to relax and spend time with their friends for a few hours each day.

After we had talked about her work for some time, she asked, "What are you doing here in India?"

I knew that Sister Veronica wasn't running her tailoring course to make good Catholics out of the Hindu and Muslim teenagers who flocked to her simple classroom every day for six months. It was an act of love. So as I explained our work, I confessed that it was hard for a lot of Christians to comprehend what we were doing in India.

"There are a couple of beautiful sermons recorded in the Bible," she replied slowly. "But in my experience, I find that preaching is usually not very effective. Your witness is your own healing journey with Jesus."

Her words resonated with me for the rest of the day. She seemed to be saying that my own needs were not at odds with the needs of others and that there was no separation between my inner life with God and my outer life in the world. Christian witness was not about arguing theological points, but about living with God and sharing that experience with others, welcoming them as companions on the journey.

* * *

The kindness of Sister Veronica and the routine of attending her tailoring classes seemed to comfort Zahera over the next few weeks, helping to take her mind off the troubles at home and the loss of her dream of finishing high school. Over the same period of time, Zahera's mother's condition seemed to stabilize—if not improve. The progression of her illness over the years had been more of a death-defying roller coaster than a downward slope, and we never knew which episode of psychosis or overwhelming physical pain might be the one to claim her life. The knowledge that her mother could die at any time cast a long shadow over Zahera's life, and during the times when her mother's health grew worse, Zahera was usually able to think of little else. Yet with each period of apparent recovery, however subtle or brief, Zahera dared to hope that her mother might one day be healthy again.

The first few weeks of the tailoring course were one of those hopeful times. But just as she began to settle into these more peaceful circumstances, Zahera was stricken with an intestinal flu which brought on days of vomiting until she could no longer keep down water, and was then followed by debilitating abdominal pain. One evening, Zahera's sister rushed into our home and begged us to help her sister. By the time we reached their house, Zahera was screaming and crying in pain, sweating profusely, and unable to stand.

Andy carried her in his arms to the road, where we laid her on a street vender's makeshift table next to a half-melted slab of ice while we waited for Zahera's mother and sister, as well as an uncle who had been summoned from the other end of the slum. They joined us on the roadside, and after flagging down a public three-wheeled taxi, we begged the driver to go straight to the hospital instead of keeping to his usual route. We positioned Zahera on the front seat, and I climbed between her and the driver so I could hold her upright while her uncle sat on the other side, nearest the open side of the vehicle. Andy climbed in the back with her mother and sister.

As we rushed toward the hospital, I tried to pray for my friend, but my thoughts were scattered and distracted by the traffic horns, Zahera's tormented sobs, and my own battle to keep from hyperventilating and breaking down from my sense of powerless fear and grief. Suddenly Zahera fell silent, and her body went limp in my arms. I put a hand to her nose and mouth, but could not feel any breath. Thinking she had died, I shook her and called out her name.

Then her uncle threw water on her face, which brought her round with a gasp and a sharp cry as she became aware once more of the pain. Before we arrived at the hospital, she collapsed a second time, and again her uncle revived her with water.

When we finally arrived at the ER, no one seemed to feel our sense of urgency. They laid Zahera out on a bed and gave her an injection of pain killer, followed by an IV drip of electrolytes, but no one examined her.

Finally, a doctor came in and pushed on Zahera's stomach, concluding that she had gastritis and warning us that she shouldn't eat until after her ultrasound. Several hours later, she was admitted to the ward, where she waited several more hours before being taken in for an X-ray.

At some point, a nurse arrived and drew blood, but no one explained what was happening. Though the ward was full of nurses, we didn't see any doctors, and the hierarchical structure of the hospital exacerbated their absence because nurses had no decision-making authority and little information about the patients under their care.

"Has her blood test come back yet?" I asked one nurse.

"Yeah, it's in her file, but that's for the doctor to see. He'll look at it and tell you the treatment."

While we waited for Zahera to be examined by the doctor, we had to keep shifting from one place to another as endless cycles of irritable cleaning staff barked at us to keep off their freshly mopped floors. In spite of their apparent zeal for spotless white tile floors, they left the bathroom untouched—an unlit, grimy closet with an ancient, gunky faucet and no soap. Though Zahera's mother was no longer delusional, she was still chronically ill and suffered from constant pain, so she was too weak to stand for more than a few minutes at a time. As the room was being cleaned, she grew tired and uncomfortable from squatting on the floor, and so she tried to get back into the room to lie down next to her daughter on the bed.

When she pushed open the door, the young man mopping the floor became incensed. "What are you doing?" he yelled. "I told all of you to get out!"

When I tried to explain the situation, he raised the mop above his head and threw it onto the ground. "You want me to stop doing my job?"

Zahera's mother turned to me and lamented, "It's all right, Umera. Let it be. It's obvious that suffering has never come near this man's house."

Her comment had the desired effect of shaming the man into relenting. "Oh, fine. Go!" he barked.

When we asked about the ultrasound, we were told that the next day was Sunday, and most of the hospital would be closed—so she would have to wait for another twenty-four hours before she could have her ultrasound or endoscopy.

When we realized that the ultrasound would be delayed, I flagged down a nurse and asked, "The doctor mentioned that my friend shouldn't eat before having her ultrasound, but then we just heard from someone else that there won't be any ultrasound until tomorrow. So is she allowed to eat now? She's hardly had anything to eat in three days—"

"How am I supposed to know who's supposed to eat what and when!" she interrupted. "You'll have to ask the doctor."

"Well, when is he coming?"

"How should I know?"

By this time, I knew that government hospitals in India—like the public schools—were only used by those who could not afford to opt for a private alternative. Because the poor were the only ones who used the government hospitals, they were treated disrespectfully and had to suffer long waits with little explanation or care. Yet they had no power to complain. And because they had received this kind of treatment their whole lives, they weren't surprised by the way they were treated. Nor did they seem fazed by the filthy conditions or the unscreened windows that let in mosquitoes at night—right in the middle of dengue season.

After Zahera was well enough to be discharged from the hospital, her lingering abdominal pain prevented her from eating anything for several days. I worried that the infection was still active and that she would slowly starve herself waiting for the pain to subside, but she gradually regained her strength.

Making sense of the suffering I witnessed in the hospital—and the suffering we continued to witness in our slum community every day—was a constant struggle. On any given day, I might find myself laughing with abandon, burning hot with rage, struck with curiosity or wonder, and sad enough to weep. Andy and I developed different ways of coping with our sorrow and confusion. At times, my interactions with suffering produced new spiritual insights or inspired deeper compassion in me, but more often the endless suffering I witnessed left me exhausted and filled me with angst, rage, and even despair. I began to be haunted by doubts about whether or not the Kingdom would actually come. And I began to ask myself if I believed in the resurrection—not just Jesus' resurrection, but the restoration of all things, the redemption of all that is evil and broken, the new creation growing out of the old. Did I still believe that good would have the final victory and that all things would be made well, even though I saw so few signs of hope in the present?

* * *

Although Zahera eventually recovered from her infection, several weeks after she returned from the hospital, her mom took a sudden downward turn. When I stopped by the house to visit, I found Zahera and her grandmother, who was visiting from the village, sitting next to Zahera's mother, who was lying on a rope bed in the alleyway in front of their house. Crying silent tears from the debilitating pain, she shook her head back and forth tremulously one moment, then, in the next, smiled at me eerily with vacant eyes like a stiff doll.

I sat next to Zahera and her grandmother as they discussed which *mazar* they should visit with Zahera's mother.

"Yes, we could take her to the *mazar*," the grandmother mused. She lived in a village nearby the shrine we were discussing. "But then, it's Muharram soon, isn't it? So there are the *tazias*. There's benefit from worshipping the *tazias*, too, so we could just wait for them to get here."

I knew that during the festival of Muharram, our neighbours would set up *tazias*—miniature buildings made of bamboo and papier–mâché —as symbols of the tomb of Muhammad's grandson Hussein, who had been killed in battle in the seventh century. Throughout the festival, people would set out food and drink before the *tazias*. At the culmination of the festival, they would carry the *tazias* in a symbolic funeral procession and then bury them in a symbolic graveyard behind the mosque.

Zahera stood abruptly and left me with her grandmother. Neighbors walked by, authoritatively offering unhelpful dietary commands about eggs, buffalo, and lentils to address the illness that was ravaging her mother's body and brain.

I got up and went inside to find Zahera, who was gathering clothes, blankets, and bags of flour and rice to take on the journey.

"Zahera, your mom's mind isn't working right now. It's dangerous to go so far away, just the two of you. What will you do if she tries to run away?"

Her eyes met mine. "What else can I do?" she asked helplessly.

I was thinking that the clear alternative would be to let her sick mother rest at home instead of taking her out of the city on public transport to go and sit in an empty shack near a Muslim saint's grave, where they both would be freezing at night and might run out of food before they were able to come back. "Has there been a benefit from going to this *mazar* in the past?" I asked.

"Yes, every time her health goes bad, we go there and she gets better," Zahera said.

All the talk about *mazars* and *tazias* and eggs made me want to bang my head against the wall, but I didn't have any helpful alternative to offer. My worldview said that Zahera's mom was suffering from a rare autoimmune disease that would one day claim her life—whether she ate eggs or not. And all my prayers to Jesus hadn't cured her either. We both knew she needed a miracle, and we were both asking for one—in our own ways—though we both also knew there were no guarantees.

* * *

While Zahera was at the *mazar*, Andy and I returned to the States to apply for new visas. For several months previous, Andy had been volunteering with a local Indian nonprofit organization to form self-help groups across the city and to begin unionizing informal workers such as street vendors and domestic workers to improve working conditions and push for fair pay. Now he would be signing on with that organization in a formal capacity, which meant applying for a more permanent visa that would allow him to work in India without having to leave every six months.

During our visit, we attended a church service, and we listened to the testimony of a young couple as they shared about their experience of God's miraculous intervention to save the life of their newborn daughter. They described the six hundred people who had all been praying for them at the same time, the nearness of God throughout the whole ordeal, the state-of-the-art medical facilities, and the world-class doctors who were involved in their daughter's treatment. I appreciated hearing an honest and personal account of a very difficult situation, and I was happy and relieved to know that their little girl was continuing to develop as a normal, healthy child.

But that story of miraculous intervention and the avoidance of tragedy also raised complex emotions and questions for me. As I sat listening to their story, I couldn't help but think of all the babies and children in my neighborhood in India who *had* died of preventable causes over the past few years—each far more simple than this baby's condition. I wondered whether those children were any less precious to God than the little girl who had been saved. I wondered whether God was really petty enough to count the number of intercessors before deciding whether or not to get involved. I wondered how people like Zahera's mom could ever capture the attention of that kind of God if they didn't have the support of six hundred people to beg for healing on their behalf.

In the American family's story, I found it remarkable that the child had survived a very serious health condition and a very rare complication after a high-risk surgery—and yet, she had been operated on by, literally, *the* best surgeon in the world. Her family could afford to take their daughter to the best medical center in the country, and they were supported by their families, who put them up in a hotel and provided for their needs while they waited for their daughter to be able to leave the hospital. Those factors of geography, income, and family connections played a significant role in determining whether that little girl would live or die.

I had waited outside of crappy public hospitals in India with families who shuttled relatives back and forth from home to bring meager provisions for the patient and the people who were waiting at their bedside. I had seen the families who came in from the villages for treatment and slept outside on the grass or curled into the fetal position on one corner of their patient's hospital bed for nights on end because there was nowhere else to stay and they had no money to pay for accommodation. I had struggled to explain lab results to Zahera and her mother in Hindi because all of their medical papers were written in a language they didn't understand, by doctors who didn't bother taking the time to communicate any of the information they contained.

Had Western Christians actually given God credit for things that were better explained by global economics, politics, or personal gain? I thought of the Indian doctors and nurses who competed for high-paying positions in American hospitals instead of taking positions at hospitals and clinics in their home country, where there are severe staff shortages. Hospitals in the U.S. can afford to pay them more, and treating wealthy patients in spacious, private offices is less stressful than treating poor patients in overcrowded clinics.

I was not resentful that many children in my home country were able to access great medical care—and I celebrated the American baby's gift of life—but I was disturbed that the children I knew in India could hardly get any medical care at all, and I grieved with the parents who had lost their children because they lacked basic medical care. For I knew that their deaths had had nothing to do with a lack of divine intervention, but rather a lack of human intervention.

Even though I knew many wealthy people in the U.S. who were extremely generous amongst their friends and relatives and were quick to respond to any need brought to their attention, the truth was that relatively few needs cropped up in their network of relationships, because everyone they knew was likely to be fairly educated, wealthy, and well-placed in the world. Yet from my time in the slums, I knew that the neediest people couldn't hope for much help when they faced crises, because they only had other needy people in their networks of relationships. That was certainly the case for Zahera and her family, whose network of relatives were scattered between the slum and the impoverished villages nearby—communities in which even the urban luxury of electricity was out of reach.

What if we could change that? I wondered. What if we, who are wealthy, could expand our circle of friends and family to include those who are poor? If a stranger needs housing, or cancer treatment, or a hot meal, we may or may not contribute through some indirect, sterile line of charitable donation. But if our sister or father or friend is the one who is ill or without a job or in need of a place to stay, there's no way we will let them go without!

The redefinition of family and responsibility for our fellow human beings was at the very heart of the Kingdom

Jesus preached. He scandalized his listeners by declaring that his mother and brother and sisters were not merely his biological kin, but included all those who did the will of God. He revolutionized our concept of the "neighbor"—whom we are to love as we love ourselves—by including not only those who are ethnically, religiously, or geographically close to us, but even those who are our enemies. Many people were offended by these teachings because they believed that Jesus was devaluing the relationships between parents and children or between people of the same nation or religion. Yet Jesus was actually telling us that we owe that same level of committed care and compassion to whomever is in need of it, whether they're biological family or not.

Life in the slum taught Andy and me that expanding our sense of family and neighborhood went beyond just moving money around. It meant making our time, energy, resources, connections, and know-how available to those whom we had accepted as part of our surrogate family. This required intentional effort and creativity because we had to reach beyond our comfort zone as we expanded our circles of friends, neighbors, and family to include people who were materially poor. Because we were in a Muslim slum, we were also intentionally including those who are often viewed by my country as enemies. Yet we believed that if we were able to begin recognizing all of our true neighbors as family, then all of the advantages we had been given in life—whether direct gifts from God or the unjust gains of an unequal system—would become blessings both to us and to neighbors like Zahera and her mother.

* * *

After Andy and I returned to India from our time in the U.S., Zahera returned to the slum from the village, where her mother continued to languish at the *mazar*, waiting for a miraculous healing. Zahera's grandmother had long since returned home to the village where she lived with Zahera's eldest uncle and his family, and Zahera had arranged for her older sister to remain at the *mazar* to care for her mother so that she herself could return to the city to care for the house (and cook for her older brother). One day during this season of reprieve, Zahera invited me to visit a Sufi saint's grave on the other side of the city with her teenage friends, who were giddy with the excitement of getting dressed up and going somewhere. I was curious to see the urban *mazar* and happy to be included in their plans, but I knew it might drag on for hours, and it would be hard for me to follow the conversation between the girls as we walked alongside noisy traffic on our way to the shrine.

The *mazar* was crammed between a large hospital complex on one side and crowded shops on the other. We passed beneath a tall, narrow archway over a small alley that led away from the busy main street into a large courtyard around the enshrined tomb. The crowded passageway was lined with beggars, and choked with visitors wearing *niqab* or prayer caps as they made their way to and from the *mazar*. All around the main shrine, a lively market had been set up, with vendors selling jewelry, street food, special handkerchiefs to place on the saint's grave, and colorful kitsch posters bearing images of chubby, pale, blue-eyed babies, or roses, or feminine hands bedecked with gold wedding jewelry and henna pressed together in greeting, or the *Ka'aba* in Mecca, or children praying *namaz*. The jewelry and the posters were all very familiar to me, since my neighbors all bought their jewelry and household decorations from *mazar* markets and religious carnivals. My companions bought a special handkerchief, and we stowed our shoes under a vendor's cart before stepping into the covered courtyard in front of the shrine.

The floor was a checkerboard of black-and-white marble tiles under a high ceiling supported by tall, white columns, and the area was packed with people—mostly women—sitting on the floor, facing the grave and praying. I was surprised to see a number of Hindu women wearing *saris* and *bindis* scattered amongst the Muslim women wearing black *niqab* or *salwar kameez* suits (long tunics worn over loose, baggy pants) with big *dupattas* draped over their heads. Running through the middle of the crowd, there was an open path leading to the steps, which climbed into the shrine itself. At the stairs, the courtyard was separated from the inner sanctum by a metal gate and a railing. Women weren't allowed beyond that point, but I could see the sepulcher draped in layers of shiny scarves and fresh flowers just a few feet ahead of us. It was covered by a small colonnade and was decorated with strings of colored lights. Men dressed in white prayer caps and *kurta-pajama* (loose-fitting white cotton tunics and trousers) walked in circles around the tomb, praying aloud.

Zahera approached the gates and tied a string to one of the bars, whispering a prayer under her breath as she did so. A grumpy looking old man with a beard and prayer cap cast her an angry glare and pointedly tore the string off the gate.

Zahera lifted her chin defiantly. Her expression evidenced neither surprise nor disappointment. "Doesn't matter," she said, loud enough for the indignant gatekeeper to hear, "The *baba* already heard my prayer."

When I asked her about it afterward, she explained that when people came to pray for something—for a healthy baby to be born, or for someone to be healed from a disease—they were supposed to tie a string onto the gate, and when their prayer was answered they should return to the *mazar* and untie the string. But you were supposed to pay some money to the *mazar* when you tied the string on and then pay more money when you took it off. Zahera didn't have the money for that.

"So that man tore off your string because you hadn't paid him any money?" I asked.

She nodded. *Yes. Exactly.*

I was infuriated that the pious, self-important Pharisaical man would try to block my impoverished friend's access to God. Guided by strict legalism and greed, he had tried to silence her prayer for her mother's recovery.

But throughout history, I knew that every religious system in the world—including my own—had tried to claim authority over God. Arrogant, self-appointed spokesmen had tried to act as the sole mediators of Her mercy and power, and tried to deny direct access to the poor—especially to women.

That telling interaction between Zahera and the gatekeeper seemed emblematic of the problem of institutionalized religion in general, which so often devolves into exclusive, hierarchical, male-dominated institutions with burdensome laws and regulations. I thought of the imams' *fatwas* (sermons) broadcast over the loudspeakers of the mosque in our neighborhood every Friday and of the fact that the women in our community were prohibited from going into the mosque—or even the graveyard. And I remembered the fiery preachers from my childhood churches and my Christian university's policy against women praying aloud during services or delivering a sermon without a man standing next to them on stage—in *California,* no less.

Throughout my time in India, it was easy for me to shake my head in disdain about how Islam had degenerated into a religion of violence, oppression, and internal strife. And at first, the long beards and black veils did stir up memories of news reports about terrorist groups or violent regimes. But then I thought of heretics being burned at the stake in medieval Europe and how the Christian faith had been divided and subdivided into myriad factions that competed and even warred against each other. This led me to acknowledge the uncomfortable fact that Islam and Christianity are quite similar in their denominational strife, their habit of persecuting and killing their mystics, their historical subjugation of women, and their penchant for forced conversion over the centuries.

Yet such abuses of power are not limited to these two religions alone. And neither Christianity nor Islam can be characterized as religions of violence or oppression, since both faiths teach about the existence of a God who engages in divine self-revelation motivated by love, and both invite human beings into an intimate relationship with this God. A beautiful saying from the Islamic tradition explains God's reason for creating the world this way: "I was a hidden treasure, and I loved to be known, and so I created the worlds both visible and invisible."[7]

While I lived in India, nearly everyone I knew was Muslim, and among them I found loyal friends, generous and courageous people, and everyday saints; regular people whose struggles and foibles were universally human. The people I met had been shaped as much by their personal life experiences and their culture as by their religion. They hoped for and feared many of the same things that my friends and family did in the West. I also came to realize that some of the most revered Muslim saints through the centuries have been women, and the Muslim world has known not only centuries of war, but peaceful centuries of scientific discovery, artistic development, and literary achievement.

As I explored my neighbors' spiritual world and reflected on my own, I began to realize that the challenge for both Muslims and Christians is to reject the harsh elements of fundamentalism, hatred, and arrogance within

---

[7] Recorded in the *Hadith Qudsi*, the extra-Qur'anic revelation.

our belief systems, which lead to violence, while clinging to the core truths of our religion, which are good, loving, and lead to beauty and wholeness in the world. Both faiths exhort people to love God and care for the poor. Both emphasize the importance of a supportive spiritual community. Both contain rich mystical traditions of prayer and direct spiritual encounters with God.

Christianity began as a small band of committed disciples, who shared their lived experience of Jesus with the world and invited others into an authentic community of radical inclusion, love, and welcome from a loving God who invited all into a Kingdom of forgiveness, peace, and reconciliation. But within a couple of centuries, that growing community of Kingdom people fell for the temptation of earthly power and influence. Christ followers were coopted by a different kind of Kingdom altogether: the Roman Empire, which instituted Christianity as the official state religion and began codifying the faith into civic law. Religious teachers became political leaders, and the Church became a hierarchical power structure that attracted people who were ambitious for wealth and influence rather than hungry for God.

The longer I lived in India and encountered the suffering of my Muslim neighbors, the more I longed to encounter that wild, loving God that the first disciples had experienced, before empire and arrogant men recast the Divine in their own image.

* * *

"How is your mom doing?" I asked Zahera one day as I sat on a low stool in her closet-sized kitchen, watching as she prepared dinner in the gathering dusk. "How much longer is she going to stay at the *mazar*?" Spices sizzled in hot oil over a single-burner gas stove on the floor in front of us.

Zahera spoke to her mom and sister by phone every few days, and she told me that her mother had begun to hear voices and see people who weren't there. "She's afraid to return home from the *mazar*, because she believes that Satan inhabits our house and is going to kill her if she stays here," she continued. "That's what the voices told her."

Her words sent a chill through me. I knew that living conditions were primitive at the *mazar*, and I worried about her mother and sister spending such a long time there alone. Yet I could also understand the intense fear that was keeping them there. I had been in the room with Zahera in the past when her mother had screamed and held terrified, one-sided conversations with a silent tormentor, staring into the corner of the room at someone none of us could see. I suggested that we spend some time praying a blessing over the house before her mother returned. "We can ask Jesus to fill the house and protect everyone who lives here," I said.

Zahera's face instantly lit up at the idea, but when the appointed day came, she cracked open the plywood door to her courtyard with a troubled expression. "We can't do it today," she told me. "I'm menstruating."

Islam is similar to Judaism in its emphasis on ritual purity, and many of the stipulations around cleanliness in the Qur'an are taken directly from the purity codes of the Jewish Torah, which is included in the Christian Bible as the first five books of the Old Testament. According to these purity codes, a menstruating woman is ceremonially unclean, and therefore isn't permitted to fast or to pray *namaz*. Zahera believed that menstruation was dirty and that it would be a sin to bring that filth into the presence of God.

I explained to her that since we would be praying to Jesus, it didn't matter whether she was on her period or not. I told her the story recorded in the gospel of Luke about the woman who had been bleeding for twelve years and had spent every last ounce of money and hope on unsuccessful medical treatment. When Jesus passed by, she touched the hem of His robe in a bid for supernatural healing. And she got it, instantly. The gospel writer records that Jesus felt the power go out of Him, and He turned to the crowd around Him to find out who had touched Him. The woman was trembling with fear, ashamed to be discovered as the unclean person with the unspeakable problem who had just contaminated this powerful, righteous teacher. But when she finally fell to her knees and confessed her unacceptable breach of decency, Jesus surprised her with a gentle response: "Go in peace, daughter. Your faith has made you well."

"We can see from this story that it doesn't matter to Jesus whether we're menstruating or not when we want to talk to Him," I told Zahera. "God made our bodies. She knows that they menstruate, and She isn't bothered by it."

Zahera smiled with relief. "So Jesus won't be angry at me?"

"Not at all," I assured her. Zahera led me into her family's main living space, a dimly lit room with a cement floor and brick walls. A younger cousin was sitting inside, and both she and Zahera covered their heads with their *dupattas* out of respect as I began praying, using whatever words came to mind. I asked for Jesus' blessing over Zahera's home and family, for peace in her mother's mind, for protection from fear and from any kind of evil that might cause them harm. We sat together on the floor for a long time, praying out loud and silently.

Afterwards, I had no way of knowing whether some demonic presence had been removed or if it had even been present in the first place. But when we finished praying, a new quality of peace and comfort had entered the room, replacing the fear and loneliness I had so often felt in that house.

Zahera was beaming. "That was wonderful," she said. "I feel so peaceful." She was excited to learn that she could always pray to Jesus, whether she was menstruating or not.

As I reflected on our interaction later, I felt certain that menstruation would never have become a spiritual impediment if the feminine elements of the Divine had been taken into account in formulating Jewish, Christian, and Islamic theology. Surely it was only a male God—or male theologians, for that matter—who would be put off by women's monthly cycles.

As I witnessed violent sexism in India and encountered the filth and shame associated with the female body, I began to wrestle more directly with the idea of a gendered God. Though the consequences of an exclusively male concept of God were more glaring in India than they had been in the West, God had been presented to me as unquestionably male throughout my childhood, and I knew that my questions and struggles went back long before I had ever been stared at and harassed by Indian men. I only had to think of my Baptist upbringing and how often girls were told that we must not arouse boys' lust with immodest clothing because it was our responsibility to "keep our brothers from stumbling."

In the same way, I saw men in India bathe publicly in wet underwear, and yet women were expected to cover their bodies to keep from arousing male lust. Even though the codes of modesty may be different in the West, the underlying framework is still the same in that it only takes male sexual desire into account. Whether women are wearing bikinis, *saris*, or *burqas*, society seems to expect them to dress with men in mind. And if the beauty of their bodies attracts unwanted, inappropriate, or abusive attention from men, women are often blamed for having provoked men's uncontrollable urges—or for causing men's "wrong seeing," as people put it in Hindi. This is the basis of rape culture all over the world.

In both societies, the core assumption is that female bodies are the problem—and the solution is to control *how much* is seen of those bodies rather than changing *how* they are seen. Men's reduction of women to sexual objects is dealt with as an inescapable problem best addressed not through inward transformation of the heart, but by covering female bodies with fabric. Because I had grown up in a thoroughly sexist society that was also deeply religious, I came to see that women will never be treated as equals—and the violence against them will never be stopped—so long as we believe that masculinity bears the image of God, but femininity does not. Eschewing the feminine aspects of God leads to a religious system in which men are considered spiritually superior to women and a culture in which they become women's social, economic, and sexual superiors as well.

This notion of male superiority in religion is not limited to Hinduism or Islam. The words of the early Church Fathers also betray sexist views that are rooted in presumptions about God's masculinity. According to St. Augustine, "Woman does not possess the image of God in herself but only when taken together with the male who is her head. . . . But as far as the man is concerned, he is by himself alone the image of God just as fully and completely as when he and the woman are joined together into one."[8] And to explain the need for women to dress modestly, Tertullian wrote,

"And do you not know that you are Eve? God's sentence hangs still over all your sex and His punishment weighs down upon you. You are the

---

[8] St. Augustine, as quoted on page 55 of *Feminist Interpretations of Augustine*, edited by Judith Chelius Stark.

devil's gateway; you are she who first violated the forbidden tree and broke the law of God. It was you who coaxed your way around him whom the devil had not the force to attack. With what ease you shattered that image of God: Man! Because of the death you merited, even the Son of God had to die . . . Woman, you are the gate to hell."[9]

These ideas mirror the Islamic concept of women being "the rope of Satan," inferior beings whose physical beauty tempts men to sin. As with sexist ideologies within Christianity, a belief in the inherent antagonism between righteousness and femininity is neither universal nor necessary to orthodox Islam, but it is certainly influential and widespread. For sexist theologians in both faith traditions, Eve's role in the Genesis narrative is taken as evidence of women's moral deficiency. Men are assumed to be the protagonists of the spiritual journey, while women are merely obstacles or helpers to them along the way. Given that these theologies have been developed exclusively by men, it comes as little surprise that they did not seek to analyze how men help or hinder women along their spiritual path, nor acknowledge the ways in which the female half of humanity images the Creator.

* * *

The house blessing seemed to put Zahera's mind at ease, but her mother and sister remained at the *mazar*, and Zahera continued to live at home by herself. Her brother would return from work late in the evenings to eat dinner and sleep, but he spent all of his free time wandering the streets with his friends, and he was neither a kind nor sociable presence in the house. Zahera continued attending

---

[9] Tertullian, *On The Apparel of Women*, Chapter 1.

tailoring classes at the convent, and occasionally I went along with her to visit with Sister Veronica.

Whenever I visited the convent, the girls clamored to talk with Sister Veronica. Depending on how her health was holding up that day, she would either join the girls in the classroom or sit in the shade outside, wearing her nun's habit and crucifix. Though she was strict and held them to high standards, she was fair and became involved in their lives when they needed help—whether that meant subsidizing the purchase of a sewing machine or helping their families to pay for emergency medical care. It was obvious that she was not building relationships with them as a tactic of manipulation, but rather out of love and care, with no expectations or strings attached.

Yet apart from the staff of a large aid organization which ran fairly ineffective poverty alleviation programs in our neighborhood, most of the local Christians I met were not interested in spending time in the slums unless they could try to evangelize my neighbors. Because they had only interacted with Muslims while handing out tracts in order to seek converts—which often generated suspicion and anger—they were often shocked when they found out that Andy and I lived in a Muslim neighborhood. "Is that safe?" they would ask. "Are they receptive?" We knew that they were really asking, "Are they receptive to Christian doctrine?"

Like so many other evangelicals, Andy and I had originally come to India imagining that we would share our faith with others in a way that would convince them to transfer their membership from the Muslim to the Christian camp. During our first months in India, one of our teammates read aloud from an article in which a Catholic priest in Pakistan reflected back on his fifty years of service in the country. In all that time, the priest said that he had seen only one conversion: his own. At the time, his perspective struck me as misguided and depressing.

But after living in India longer and getting to know my Muslim neighbors, I began to appreciate his observation, for I could recognize the ways that my relationships and experiences were slowly changing my perspectives, theological beliefs, and behavior. I imagined that my own slow conversion into the image of Christ would take a lot longer than fifty years.

I also began to wonder if conversion for my neighbors might mean growing spiritually and even drawing closer to Christ, but without ever leaving the fold of Islam. We had seen so many ways in which God was already at work in people's lives through their own faith tradition, answering their prayers and cultivating compassion. Like iron sharpening iron, perhaps God was using us for one another's conversions—not into each other's religions, but into deeper love, joy, peace, patience, kindness, goodness, gentleness, and self-control. Perhaps we were being drawn into deeper forgiveness, peace-making, justice-seeking, and courage.

We had also come to doubt that a loving God would sentence millions of impoverished Muslim children, women, and men to eternal damnation simply because they grew up calling God by a different name and had never met another Christian or read a Bible. (Most of our friends couldn't even read.) And we also realized that Jesus said much more about loving one's enemies, living with humility, lifting up the oppressed, and sacrificing oneself on behalf of others than he ever said about persuading others to believe the same doctrines.

As my understanding of "Christian witness" shifted, I became annoyed with other Christians' assumptions about what Andy and I were up to in the slum. If we talked about building relationships or trying to learn about the needs of the community, fellow Christians often nodded their heads and observed, "I see. Building trust. Good strategy—later they'll be receptive to your message." Everything seemed to be cloak-and-dagger evangelism. But then I met Sister Veronica, who simply *loved* the girls who came to her school. Her life and work affirmed my growing desire to love my neighbors without holding onto an ideological agenda, and it was hugely comforting to encounter a kindred spirit who did not view my life in India with suspicion or judgment.

* * *

Our decision to move into a slum had been a huge leap of faith, a choice to live in hope that God would bring about transformation. It was a declaration that we were so convinced that change was coming that we were willing to stay there until it happened. I knew that as our neighbors struggled with hunger, sickness, abuse, and systemic injustice, they often felt hopeless about things ever changing. But during that somber season of confusion and upheaval, it occurred to me that in Mark chapter 2, when the paralyzed man was lowered down to Jesus through the roof of a packed house in Palestine, he was healed because of his *friends'* faith.

In that moment, the paralyzed man may not have been confident of being healed, but his friends took drastic action in the hope that he would be. Perhaps his own mind had been ablaze with fear and skepticism, but that mustard seed of faith from his friends was enough. And I wondered if maybe that was the kind of faith that Andy and I could hold on our neighbors' behalf in the slum. If there were even just two people out of the thousands in our neighborhood who believed that transformation was possible, who held onto hope for the lives of Zahera and her family, could that be a mustard seed that would eventually grow into a wild, vibrant mustard plant and offer shelter to others in its branches? I was living on the assumption that it was.

9

FREEDOM TO LOVE

Winter 2013–2014

"But she is with everyone and in everyone, and so beautiful is her secret that no person can know the sweetness with which she sustains people, and spares them in inscrutable mercy."

— Hildegard of Bingen

When Andy and I returned to the States in December 2013 to apply for a permanent work visa, the application process turned out to be very complicated. For several weeks, we were left in suspense while we waited for our paperwork to be approved or denied. As the processing time dragged into January, the slow, unstructured days gave me a lot of time to marinate in my own thoughts. To be honest, I wasn't sure if I really wanted those visas to come through, or not.

The weather was cold, and we spent our days in my parents' house under grey skies that suggested perpetual morning or evening, but never midday when life really gets going. My mind and body seemed to be in a fog. If I bundled up next to the heater, I felt lethargic, yet the cold paralyzed me. My fatigue scared me. No matter how much I slept, waking to my alarm wrenched me out of a deep REM cycle. I wanted to rest, and I knew that I needed to, but I worried that I would never feel energetic again.

During the weeks we spent waiting for a response from the visa office, I went to counseling to talk through my emotional exhaustion and the anxiety I was feeling about the social obligations of our life in the slum. The stress of living in this environment was augmented by the fact that our neighbors' culture and language lent themselves to making requests in a highly emotional, assertive, and relentless way. As we had learned the language, Andy had actually found this aggressive, direct form of expression liberating—he was able to assert himself more in Hindi than he had ever had in English, and gradually he began to carry this freedom into his English-speaking life. But I agonized about the thought that I might fail to meet people's expectations, and I felt guilty about saying no to people who had such significant, glaring needs. In America, I had never thought of myself as a person who had trouble saying no. But in India, I found it nearly impossible to set the boundaries I needed in my friendships with neighbors, which led me to cave in, or avoid direct confrontation by making excuses, or eventually just stay home.

If I went several days without seeing Amna, she would show her disapproval by making an angry face and asking where I had been and why I hadn't come over. Other times, when I would get up to leave from her house, she and her daughters would get angry and say, "Sit down! Why do you have to go?" I knew that these antics, albeit somewhat manipulative, came from a place of love. They genuinely wanted to spend time with me.

I also knew that Indian hospitality demanded that the hosts act offended if their guests ate "too little" or left "too early," and my role was to be equally persevering in extricating myself. I had also seen through Amna's harsh exterior enough times to know that anger was often her only means of expressing her hurt or desires. But I still found the process exhausting, and I hated to disappoint my friends. I didn't know how to explain that while our long visits were relaxing for them, they required energy from me. Especially after a full day of visiting several families in the community, I needed time to be by myself and rest.

Yet my guilt was not limited to disappointing people. I also felt guilty about having more freedom than my neighbors did. Whenever I visited Zahera's house, the whole family would be sad about her mother's illness, and Zahera would either be stressed out or bored from having nothing to do but sit inside all day. I always felt terrible about leaving: it was so easy for me to step out of the situation whenever I wanted, but she was stuck. I felt like I was abandoning Zahera, especially if she asked me to stay. Knowing how hard my neighbors' lives were in comparison with mine made it difficult for me to justify setting boundaries or saying, "no." What right did I have to separate myself from their problems?

I also compared myself directly with my friends in the slum, feeling that I should be able to adjust myself completely to their culture. If they weren't bothered by open-ended social engagements with no fixed starting or finishing time, then why was I? If they never needed time alone, then why did I? Many times, when I would shut the door to our room to pray or journal at our desk, our current landlady, Yazmin, and her toddler, Firoz, would come upstairs to see me. Despite the closed door, they would come over to the window (which was nearly always kept open for ventilation) and either start a conversation or just climb into the room and ask what I was doing. At those moments, I felt pressure to spend time with them instead of "selfishly" continuing what I was doing. After all, hadn't I moved into the slum to spend time with people?

My counselor helped me to see that setting boundaries was not selfish, but healthy—quality time with my neighbors could only be sustained by energizing myself with the rest and solitude that I needed. She also pointed out that I couldn't help the fact that my life was different from the lives of the people around me. I could empathize with them in their struggles, but a crisis in Zahera's family didn't negate my own need to make dinner, sleep, or continue my own life. She also suggested that instead of viewing all our differences as areas in which I needed to become more like my neighbors, I could look for ways to hold onto my own culture and introduce something useful to my Indian friends. I could certainly learn from Yazmin to hold my schedule more loosely and to value relationships over tasks, but perhaps Yazmin could learn from me about taking time to explore her own thoughts and feelings.

These conversations revealed how I had been ignoring my own limitations and needs as a person and also feeling overly responsible for the people around me. I realized that setting better boundaries was part of the messy, awkward process of empowering people to take care of themselves instead of encouraging dependency. Yet I also knew that it would be hard to implement these changes once we returned to India—and no matter how hard I tried, I would continue to be plagued by feelings of guilt and anxiety.

I began to fantasize about Andy and I having our own apartment, sleeping-in together, and enjoying a Saturday in the seclusion of a home where no one would come to the door. I dreamed of wearing jeans and sundresses and living in a more temperate climate. I also worried that I might end up cutting my life short or being chronically ill because of my nearly constant battle with parasites.

"God, I want joy out of life," I wrote in a moment of raw honesty. "I want rest and fun and enjoyment and connection with other people . . . I want to be faithful to You, but right now I'm looking at others who love You and have it easier than me and I'm wondering, would you let me live like that?"

Meanwhile, Andy was eager to continue his work with the NGO and felt anxiety over the possibility of being separated from the people in the neighborhood where he had made a home. There was tension between us because we were not in the same place emotionally. Andy was concerned for my well-being, and I wanted him to be happy and fulfilled, but it was hard to support one another during that period of waiting when we knew that our hearts were pulling us in different directions.

One Sunday morning while Andy and my family were at church, I sat in my childhood bedroom alone, taking advantage of the empty house to spend some time with the question that I had been afraid of asking. I felt responsible for continuing what I had started in India, but I was also weary from long months of trauma, stress, poor health, discomfort, loneliness, and inner struggle. I felt paralyzed about making a decision and terrified of being told what to decide. If God asked me to stay in the slum, I would feel trapped, and my struggles would continue. But if God asked me to leave, then I would have failed. I tried to quiet myself to listen.

"What do you want me to do?" I asked.

The voice from within startled me: *What do you want?*

"I don't know," I replied. "Why should I stay?"

To be with me. To love me. To love your neighbors. What kind of tree are you? There's more than one place you can grow.

"You aren't going to tell me what to do?"

You have freedom. There are good possibilities in both directions.

"But that freedom is crushing me!"

Why?

"Because I'm afraid of failing. Or choosing the wrong thing."

But there's not a wrong choice.

"I'm afraid of disappointing myself and others. I want to leave India, but I want to do something important with my life."

You don't need to worry about disappointing other people. You don't need to be a hero. You don't need to measure up to others.

"There is so much injustice and so many people who need help there. I've already spent so much time learning Hindi and getting to know people—I don't want that to be a waste."

Your leaving wouldn't be a waste. But it's not over yet. Do you love India?

I knew that I did not. I didn't love the conservative culture or the festivals or the meat market or the trash heaps or the weather. I realized that the excitement of a foreign place was no longer enough to keep me there. "Perhaps that's how it always is with me," I mused. "When I reach the end of my idealism, I want to leave."

Might that happen anywhere?

I knew that my idealism wouldn't sustain me anywhere. I would have to face boredom and restlessness, injustice, discouragement, and the slow pace of change— if it came at all—anywhere I planted myself. But I felt I would have more resources with which to confront those things if I lived somewhere other than India. Maybe I would have a church community, a wider circle of friends, places and ways to relax and sometimes distract myself.

India is not the only place you can find me. I care more about you than anything you do. I have compassion on you. I see your distress. I know this has been a strain.

I thought back to the discernment retreat when our team had prayerfully decided to move from Delhi to Ilahabad. I recalled the purpose and anticipation I had felt as we contemplated our future there. We had sensed the possibility of so many great things happening if we went, and now I felt confused about what that sense of direction from God had really meant—or whether it had been true at all. I asked God about that.

Those things have happened. Think of all the love you have shown, the welcome you've received, the friendships that have formed.

I pictured the smiling mothers and children while I played and talked with them. I pictured Andy and me standing up for the thief in front of the angry crowd. I remembered countless trips to the hospital, interventions in domestic violence, conversations with people who were despairing and alone.

Wonderful things can happen through you wherever you go, but there's more to come if you stay.

"You're giving me freedom to choose, but I feel like you have a preference."

I don't want to control you.

"What do you want me to do?" I asked, annoyed by God's evasive answer.

You won't be more effective anywhere else than you are right now—but other places will be easier for you.

God was giving me the freedom to make a decision based on what was sustainable, yet She also warned me that I shouldn't fool myself into thinking that I could be more effective somewhere else. Working toward change is always slow and difficult, but I had deep, loving relationships with people in my community, and that was significant and worthwhile.

After it became clear that I had complete freedom, and either path could lead to good and fruitful outcomes, I felt confused rather than relieved. I prayed for help to overcome my fears of failure and of disappointing others. I thanked God for the freedom She had extended to me and asked for the humility and courage to accept it. I recognized that freedom as an extraordinary act of love, and it was a huge weight off my shoulders to know that God wasn't angry at me or pressuring me with any expectations of Her own. These realizations freed me to contemplate the future without guilt or fear, and this deeper knowledge seemed more important than the decision itself.

So I didn't make a decision—not then. About a week later, I realized that my heart had quietly decided to return to India and try out this new freedom. While I had been hanging in mental limbo, I had begun to wonder whether my uncertainty or unwillingness to return to India was actually holding up the visa process. Was God waiting for me to decide to move forward before making it legally possible for me to do so? I still don't know the answer to that question, but our visas were approved soon after I made my decision.

* * *

When we landed in Delhi that February, I noticed the usual things first: the crowds, the grime, the thick smoke hanging in the air from the little fires everyone burned at that time of year to keep warm. I knew that the area around the train station wasn't a fair representation of India, because parts of the country were beautiful, peaceful, and clean, but this was the gritty neighborhood where we took a small, dingy hotel room to await the departure of our train a day and a half later. The train to Ilahabad was delayed as usual, but this time we had bunks to ourselves and the car wasn't nearly as crowded as the one that had taken us to Delhi two months before. I felt irritated by the delay and by the grimy railway station platform where we had to wait before boarding the train. I was also irritated when someone stole Andy's shoes while we were sleeping on the train, so that on arrival the next morning, he walked off the train barefoot like an Indian holy man.

But as we left the train station, I felt my spirits lifting in spite of myself. It was sunny and cool, and as we sped along in the autorickshaw, I had to smile at the familiar scenes of street life that we breezed past: chai stands, laborers waiting for work, goats, cows, rickshaws, and pedestrians everywhere—chaotic and pulsing with life, the way that all of India was, with an energy that made me excited and made me want to be part of it all. It was less crowded and more laid-back than in Delhi. And the sky was actually blue.

Then we were back in our community. We were greeted with smiles and laughter as we held new babies that had been born while we were away. We somberly received news about the old men who died in our absence. People were happy, people were sad; some were healthy and some were sick. Everyone had engagements, sorrows, and secrets to tell us about, and we were energized to be part of it all again as our friends told us how much they had missed us and how glad they were that we were back. Our landlord's two-year-old son, Firoz, had started talking since we had left, and one of the few words he had learned was Andy's name. He had apparently begun calling it at our door while we were gone, and now that we were back, he happily yelled it up the stairwell whenever we were home.

I felt a sense of belonging that I had missed without even realizing that the longing was there. I made *roti* in my simple kitchen, looking at the bright colors of the fresh green peppers, orange lentils, and red and yellow spices sitting in glass jars on my counter. I savored the familiar sound of the call to prayer. I rediscovered the taste of chai with salt. I wrapped my tongue around those strange Hindi d's and r's as I remembered words and names that had grown dim during our time in the States. At first, I wondered how we had ever slept through all the night noises, but then I did. I felt a sense of peace and gratitude that I hadn't felt for a very long time, even before we had left for the States.

For in spite of my stressful experiences in India and my uncertainties about what the future would hold and my doubts about how much I could handle, I knew that I really *wanted* to be back in this community—not out of duty, guilt, fear, or anything else, but out of love. I wanted to see some of my hopes for our community realized. I wanted to be there for people over time. I wanted to press on, for the first time in my life, past the restlessness, boredom, difficulties, and frustrations that tempted me to distract myself with something new and exciting. I wanted to experience the deeper joy of committing to a particular place and a particular people over the long haul. I wanted to stick around long enough for *me* to actually change instead of just opting for a change of scenery. So we were back in our "village" again, and this time it felt like a gift.

10
MEENA

Fall 2013–Spring 2014

"Growth begins when we start to accept our own weakness."

— Jean Vanier

Once I decided that I could joyfully return to India with Andy and continue my life in the slum without a sense of divine obligation, I was genuinely happy to be there. But although I enjoyed many meaningful, enjoyable moments with our neighbors, our days remained intense, and as my struggles resurfaced, I began to feel overwhelmed, discontent, burdened by my neighbors' pain and by the responsibilities I took on through my involvement in their lives. Though I had returned to India in freedom, I was still confused and disappointed with myself. I had high ideals, but my daily life felt tedious as I went through the rounds of visiting people and making conversation. I was exhausted by my role as listener and helper, forever asking questions and trying to solve problems and support others in their times of distress. That care and energy so rarely flowed back toward me, and I felt tired, uncared for, burnt out, lonely.

* * *

November 2013

I met Meena several months before my trip to the States to apply for new visas. I had been sitting at a friend's open-air shop when she came over and stood somewhat timidly next to the jars of sweets, chewing tobacco, and lentils. I didn't know her well, but she was easily the smallest woman on the alleyway. She walked with a limp due to a Polio-affected leg, and I had seen her husband in a drunken rage more than once. I remembered one incident several months earlier when, in the middle of the day, she and her children huddled against the wall inside their house as her husband kicked them. Meanwhile, I had stood outside with the neighbors, watching in horror, uncertain what to do. I had no relationship with anyone in their family, and I knew that publicly shaming an abuser could lead him to take out his embarrassment and anger on his family with even more violence later.

That day at the shop, I noticed a long, deep cut on Meena's forearm that was just starting to heal. When I asked her about it, she told me that her husband had cut her with a knife during a recent fight. Right away, the shop owner's twelve-year-old daughter chimed in with the gory details of what the wound had looked like immediately afterward. Obviously, this story was already common knowledge among the people who lived on that alley, and it had likely happened in full view of the neighbors. I expressed concern, and Meena told me that her husband,

Iqbal, "fought" with her every day and that she was often unable to prepare meals for the family because he blew so much of his meager earnings on alcohol.

Meena told me that after her husband had stabbed her, she had gone to the police station for help, and the police had come to her house to arrest him. But after making Iqbal sign a report about the incident with his thumbprint, they just sent him back home.

"Come, sit down," Meena said, leading me outside the shop. I sat down on a chicken coop, and she seated herself on a plastic chair in front of me. I thought she was going to talk more about what had happened with her husband, but she completely dropped the subject and began aggressively demanding that I help her obtain a voter ID card and a different category of ration card so that she would be eligible for more help from the government each month. I didn't understand which documents she already had, and she didn't understand that I couldn't help her without more complete information.

After arguing for some time about what I was able to do, I brought the conversation back to the violence in her home. I explained that it didn't matter how many kilos of rice or flour she was eligible for each month if she and her children were living in constant terror. I took Meena's hand and motioned toward the fresh scar on her arm.

"I'm worried about this right now," I told her. "About what your husband is doing to you."

As Meena's demeanor shifted, I invited her to come with me to a women's help center the following Monday to figure out her options. I confirmed a time and then got up to head to a women's self-help group that was meeting down the street.

"Wait," she said, pulling me back down.

"What is it?" I asked.

"I know he could kill me," Meena said, starting to cry. "I'm so worried, but where can I go?"

"There's a house here in the city, where women can go to stay if it's not safe for them at home," I told her.

"What about my children?"

"They can go with you. Or if your husband goes to jail, you can live here safely. Come with me on Monday, and they'll explain what your options are. Things are bad right now, but there's hope. You can change things. There are women at this office who have also made new lives for themselves."

Though everything I told Meena was based on what I had heard from the lawyers who worked at the women's rights organization where I volunteered, I soon realized that I had been naïve in my assumption that Meena and her three young daughters would be able to access shelter, legal help, and police protection. The police responsible for reporting crime and arresting perpetrators, along with the judges who preside over cases of rape and domestic abuse—not to mention the codes of Indian law themselves—all approach the problem of violence against women from a male point of view. Unfortunately, this means that they are largely unresponsive to women's needs. Furthermore, because women often have little or no support network outside their family, they are dependent on the very people who abuse them. As an Indian human rights lawyer once told me, "Most Indian women would rather put up with violence than be alone." She was a well-educated, confident campaigner for women's rights, yet she admitted that she herself would likely put up with a measure of abuse in exchange for some semblance of security and a respectable place in society.

In Meena's tragic circumstances, I saw the practical results of women being made to feel alienated from God, because as we talked through her options, she emphasized again and again that divorce was not among them.

"But why not?" I pushed.

"Because it's a sin. God would be angry."

"God cares about your safety and the well-being of your children. God is angry about the way that your husband is mistreating all of you—*that* is sin."

I wanted so badly for her to understand that God was on her side, but because her views of God had been influenced by earthly fathers, authorities, and religious leaders, she had drawn the conclusion that God was just one more angry man, indifferent to her pain and more concerned with his own power than with anything or anyone else.

Although Meena was unwilling to file for divorce, she bravely visited the women's help center with me to learn about her options. When Meena and I first arrived at the office with two of her little girls in tow, the staff learned that none of them had eaten all day and graciously sent for plates of *sabzi-puri* (curried vegetables and deep-fried bread) for them to eat while they waited. But when the counselor finally arrived, Meena got sidetracked from her story and kept asking about some mythical medicine that wives could secretly crush into a husband's food to help him give up an alcohol addiction.

"I've seen the commercial on TV. It comes in a container this big," she said, measuring with her hands.

The counselor raised her eyebrows and looked at me questioningly.

"Meena, I don't think there is such a medicine," I said gently. "I don't think that will work."

"But it will! You know Rubina, who lives down the street? Her husband used to be even worse than mine! But then she started putting this medicine in his food every day, and he stopped drinking. She's the one who told me about it."

I sat back helplessly. It was reasonable for her to hope that some magic potion from a medicine man would solve her problems, since there didn't seem to be any other workable options on the table.

"I don't know anything about a medicine like that," the

counselor said in a politely polished-over tone of frustration. "But what we can offer you here is mediation or legal help." Clearly, the counselor was not used to dealing with uneducated people.

Although Meena was unprepared to pursue a divorce at that stage, the women's rights organization wanted to inform her about the full range of options, so a lawyer spoke briefly with her about how to file legal proceedings against her husband. He told her that in order to file for a divorce, she would need to take time off—from the house where she worked as domestic help—to appear in court hearings over the next year or two. He explained to me that it would be difficult for Meena to understand the proceedings, much less afford the court fees.

I asked how she and her children could continue to live with Iqbal's drunken rage during the years it would take to get a divorce—if she ever decided she wanted one. I asked where they would go after the divorce if Meena's husband was unwilling to leave the makeshift house they currently shared. There didn't seem to be good answers to either of these questions. In a country where a man stabbing his wife didn't land him in jail—even if she reported it to the police while the open wound was still bleeding—divorce seemed like the only option for guaranteeing the safety of Meena and her children. Yet because of their poverty, divorce was hardly an option at all.

So the counselor and the lawyer proposed social mediation with Meena's husband. They had discovered that sending an official letter to an abusive husband, summoning him to their office for mediation, and threatening him with legal action if his abusive behavior continued, was sometimes an effective way of ensuring a woman's safety within her marriage.

I was doubtful that such a strategy would work in Meena's case, since her husband scarcely seemed to be in his right mind, and I had never seen him sober. Still,

Meena seemed excited about the idea, since it was something concrete she could do to take control of the situation, and I knew she still held out hope that Iqbal could be miraculously reformed. The organization's willingness to get involved was a significant affirmation of the legitimacy of her pain and her need for safety, so I wasn't about to try to talk her out of it.

"How old are you?" the counselor asked, pen poised over the paper on her clipboard.

"How old am I?" Meena repeated. She laughed. "How should I know!"

The counselor seemed to lose patience with Meena's rough village dialect and manners. "Can you help her with this?" she asked, handing me the clipboard. "We need her name, age, address, and a record of every instance of abuse from the time she got married until now, with all the facts: dates, children's ages, and a description of everything that's happened."

The counselor left the room, and I spent the next two hours interviewing Meena about her life, trying to construct a linear report out of the circular narrative of her recollections. I estimated her children's ages, her wedding date, and other points on her timeline by asking questions like, "Was that before or after *Eid*?" or, "In the rainy season or the hot season?"

It was a strange experience to realize that I was much more comfortable interacting with my neighbor than the high-caste Hindu staff of the women's help center. It wasn't just a matter of understanding her accent—it was a matter of understanding how her mind worked, of entering into her experience. What the staff lacked was not any kind of special *ability* so much as a *desire* to relate to her. It angered me that even within an organization ostensibly committed to women's rights and equality, the prejudice against poor, uneducated women remained. If Meena was excluded even here, then who *would* advocate for her—or for the vast majority of the women in India?

I was worried about whether the letter might make Meena's husband even angrier by letting him know that she had approached a lawyer about his abuse. But with daily violence already the norm, it was hard to imagine things getting worse. Neither Meena nor her daughters were safe as it was, and so we agreed to keep our trip to the women's help center a secret and planned for Meena to act surprised when the letter came in the mail.

Because Meena had no real address, the letter was simply marked with her husband's name, the Hindi word for "shack," and the name of the slum. When the mailman delivered the letter, he carried it around the neighborhood, asking where Iqbal who lived in the shack was. When the letter finally made it into Iqbal's hands, a crowd of curious and somewhat alarmed neighbors arrived with it, accompanying the mailman. Iqbal was illiterate and had never received anything in the mail, so everyone sensed trouble and guessed that the letter must have come from the police. Iqbal already had a long history of being "warned" by police or being taken into custody following an incident of violence, though he had always been released without further consequence.

As the crowd held the letter aloft, looking for someone who could read it, Meena snatched the letter out of a neighbor's hands and waved excitedly for me to come over. "The letter came!" she called out gleefully. So much for acting surprised.

I had hoped that the neighbors would track down some other educated resident of our neighborhood to read the letter so that I wouldn't be linked to the process Meena had initiated with the women's rights center, but Andy and I were both visiting friends on her alley when the mail came. She handed us the letter, and everyone waited expectantly as though we were about to deliver a public service announcement.

"This is really Iqbal's personal business," Andy told the crowd. "Why does everyone else need to know what his letter says? Let's go read this inside," he said to Iqbal, motioning toward their small makeshift room.

We ducked under the low doorway and sat down on the dimly lit *taakat* inside with Meena and Iqbal. She was exultant; he was temporarily lifted from his usual intoxicated stupor into wide-eyed terror, stuttering and slurring questions at lightning speed and pleading with Andy not to let the cops take him away.

Andy tried to calm him down long enough to hear what was actually in the letter. "It's not from the cops. But it *is* from an organization that helps women, and they can have the police arrest you if you continue to drink and hurt your family. They've come to know about what's happening, and they want you and Meena to come to their office to talk about it."

"Let's go. Right now," Meena said authoritatively to Iqbal, jumping up from the *taakat*.

"No, no, in the letter they've set a time for you to meet them—on Wednesday," I said. "You have to wait until then."

We explained firmly that Iqbal must be sober in order to visit the office, and his fear of police and the whole hazy constellation of authority figures this letter represented drove him to promise that he would be. We all hoped that his instinct for self-preservation would carry him through to Wednesday.

It didn't. On Wednesday afternoon, when Andy and I arrived to take Meena and Iqbal to the office, he was as drunk as ever. Meena was undeterred, limping determinedly out the door and yelling to Iqbal that if he didn't come with her she would divorce him.

I followed her outside. "Meena, we really can't bring him to the office like this. He's not in his right mind. The staff won't allow him to be there."

"I'm going to divorce him," she hollered again.

Now Iqbal was stumbling out of the house to follow us. "Stop! Come back here!" he bellowed.

Andy stood beside him, trying to reason with him. When Iqbal began to run after us, Andy blocked his path.

"Are you sure you want a divorce?" I asked Meena as we made our way toward the main road. "You know that they can't do the mediation today without Iqbal."

"He'll come," she said, her eyes shining with hope.

"He can't come. He's drunk," I repeated.

"Then I'll divorce him," she said again.

I felt encouraged that she seemed to have reached the point of realizing it was unlikely for her husband to change. "Okay," I told her. "If that's what you want, then I will go with you."

We crossed the road and I started to wave down a taxi, but Meena continued to look across the road expectantly. "Wait," she said suddenly. She started to cross back toward the slum.

"Meena, we need to go before he gets up here!" I called as I began to follow her back across four lanes of traffic. I imagined that we had a limited amount of time to leave before Iqbal broke free of Andy or whoever else might be restraining him at that point.

But Meena had no intention of going to the office without her husband, much less of divorcing him. She had only hoped her bluff would be enough to scare him into transforming himself into the husband and father she needed him to be. The shining in her eyes turned to disappointment as she stared forlornly down the path where we had left Iqbal. We stood together silently, lost in our own thoughts.

"Do you want to come to my house for tea?" I asked after a moment.

Her eyes widened in surprise. "In *your* house?" she asked.

My nod brought an embarrassed smile to her face. She was, perhaps, the poorest individual in our community, and she still viewed me as a sort of patron on par with the wealthy people whose houses she cleaned. Perhaps my desire for equal friendship instead of deference struck her as a lack of propriety or as just plain ignorance about the way these things usually worked. Nonetheless, Meena agreed, somewhat reluctantly, to come over. As I prepared tea, she seated herself on the *taakat*, looking around the room in wonderment at the brick walls, cement floor, overhead fan, and rack of dishes that must have seemed so luxurious in comparison with her own home. Now *I* felt embarrassed by how much all of it impressed her.

Meena sat in my room for two hours, unloading her pain, trying on possibilities, and voicing her fears. Meanwhile, in her shack, Andy sat with the broken man she was married to, laying out hard truths in his calm, gentle way. A few days later, when Iqbal became the victim of other men, who made a habit of harassing him while he was drunk, Andy defended him and encouraged the men to give him a chance to change instead of adding to the frustration and anger that would inevitably be taken out later on his wife and their three small children.

***

February 2014

The next time Meena visited my house, the two of us were alone inside when Iqbal showed up at the door, belligerently drunk, and yelled unintelligibly until she left with him. My landlady was so frightened by the incident that she no longer wanted to let Meena come into our house. With both mediation and divorce off the table as immediate solutions, I began asking around about a safe place for her to go.

Then one day, a neighbor stopped by to tell me that Iqbal had died.

"The Iqbal who is married to Meena?" I asked. "Are you sure?"

She nodded soberly. "Iqbal who was here at your house."

She explained that he had collapsed in his shack early that morning and then had died at the hospital a couple of hours later. She said that some neighbors were saying it was a heart attack, but others were saying that his fear of the police had killed him.

I worried that Meena would be blamed for his death—and that perhaps Andy and I would be implicated as well.

By the time I reached Meena's shack, Iqbal's body had already been brought back from the hospital and was laid on a *taakat* outside. I watched their neighbors put up a white funeral tent, set out chairs, and light incense next to his head. Meena and her two younger daughters were gathered around his body, crying, as the oldest girl, who was eight years old, swatted at the flies with a piece of cloth.

I knew that Iqbal's death would make things easier for Meena and her girls; in fact, this may have been the only way they would have ever been rescued from the hellish situation they were in. Yet I also knew that it was not easy to be a widow in India—and I couldn't help wondering if Meena was sobbing over the body of her tormenter because of the loss of status and the hardship she knew she would now face without a man to head her household. In some ways, Iqbal's death was a mercy—and yet even as that thought swam into my mind, I knew that his death was not God's doing. Iqbal had most likely destroyed himself through his alcohol addiction.

When Iqbal's parents arrived from a nearby slum, I noted that his father looked like an older, bearded version of his son—and he showed up dead drunk. Some of the other men had to drag him away from the funeral when he began cursing his son and reached out to touch the body, perhaps to dishonor it in some way. Through that small window into Iqbal's childhood, we began to see Iqbal as the product of a destructive cycle rather than an incomprehensibly violent person. Trauma had been passed from one generation to the next like an heirloom, each child learning cycles of violence instead of the letters of the alphabet.

We were disturbed by the way Iqbal's life ended with no apparent redemption in the arc of his story. His death reminded me how quickly grief and loss could completely change life, stealing away loved ones, taking away the relationships and routines that make up the day-to-day fabric of our existence. I was sobered by the reality that whether we died young and unexpectedly or old and boney, death was unavoidable. I had approached life as a project, planning out the arc of my years—what I would accomplish, where I would go, who I would become. Yet life was not about what I created for myself, but about what had been given to me—and how I chose to respond.

Knowing that Iqbal's widow was penniless, the neighbors pooled money to pay for the tent and the large pots of food that were customarily prepared by the family of the deceased for the funeral guests. They sent young men from the community to inform all of Iqbal's relatives around the city. Even though Iqbal had not been well-liked, our poor neighbors extended themselves to provide for an even poorer family in their midst.

Before long, however, it seemed that in all their reverence for the dead, everyone had forgotten who this man had been while he was alive. Within hours of his heart attack, general consensus grew around the idea that Iqbal had died "from fear of the police."

"Over the last couple of months with his wife going to visit lawyers and occasionally going or threatening to go to the police station for help, the poor man must have lived in constant anxiety!" I overheard them say.

So the story went, and its subtext was clear: it was Meena's fault for trying to get help, and other women in similar situations had better suffer in silence—they don't want their husbands to end up dead, do they?

I understood why our neighbors—including the women—were blaming Meena for Iqbal's death: by denying the truth, they could ignore the gravity of the addictions and violence in their own families. Even if they would continue to suffer violence in their own families as a result, upholding the status quo was a safer path than opposing it. I also knew that in India, the man is the head of the house, and he has the authority to beat his wife and children. If a woman raises her voice in opposition to his power, then she is shaming the family, and she needs to get in line. Nevertheless, Andy and I worked hard to help dispel this rumor, and the blaming voices eventually quieted down.

* * *

For the next forty days after Iqbal's death, our neighbors believed that his spirit remained in the house before moving on to the next realm. Every day during that time, Meena had to perform a *fatiya*, a special prayer made along with offerings of incense and food. Meena told me that every night, as she lay awake worrying, her husband would appear at the foot of their bed. He would call out the girls' names and try to nudge them awake. Sometimes, if she managed to fall asleep, his voice would wake her up. Yet these nighttime visits seemed to comfort her, and she described them to me in the morning with a wistful smile.

The man who visited at night sounded so different from the violent, drunken man who had lived with her before. His spirit did not stumble or slur or yell in anger. It could be that these were merely hallucinations caused by grief and wishful thinking. Or perhaps this *was* Iqbal: relieved of his body and the alcohol that had flooded it, perhaps his spirit was able to see things more clearly. Perhaps now he was able to feel genuine love for his family and to understand the ways he had added to their misery.

Though I wanted to believe in a redemptive end to Iqbal's story, I wondered if some of Meena's apparent happiness about these "visits" was just her way of putting on a brave face, or clinging to a scrap of comfort amidst her terrifying new circumstances. One morning, when I asked whether she had been visited the night before, she responded defensively, *"Kahan hame der lage?*—Why would I be afraid? I wasn't afraid."

I knew other people who *were* afraid of these kinds of visits. They didn't believe that the men they had loved and known were coming to spend more time with them, but that the spirits of their dead husbands were coming back to claim their other half.

* * *

Shortly after Iqbal's death, hunger drove Meena to return to her job cleaning house for a wealthy woman in a neighborhood nearby. Even though the woman had promised Meena that she could have her job back after the mourning period was over—and though Meena tried to return to work long before her forty days of mourning had ended—someone else had been permanently hired in her place.

As soon as possible after Iqbal's death, Andy and I started the process of trying to help Meena apply for a widow's pension from the government. It wouldn't be enough money for the family to live on comfortably, but it would be a safety net—something to keep them afloat during times of unemployment, or to pay for school fees and clothing at times when Meena's low-paying cleaning jobs were covering the cost of meals. Yet in the end, the bureaucratic process surrounding the widow's pension seemed to have been designed to prevent the neediest widows from accessing it: Meena had to present documents that she didn't have and couldn't get because she didn't have other documents. After months of effort, she was never issued an official I.D., and so she could never apply for her widow's pension.

While we were navigating the bureaucracy of the widow's pension, Meena set out to look for work every day, traveling slowly from house to house on foot. According to custom, her in-laws should have been providing food for her during the mourning period, but they had stopped bringing over meals after a few days. A compassionate neighbor who was also a widow empathized with Meena's situation and shared food with her family whenever she could. Andy and I also gave Meena a bit of money here and there to keep her going, but these sporadic gifts were not an income, and they couldn't carry her forever. Often, she and her three daughters went hungry.

Meanwhile, Andy and I searched for a job for Meena, but with an endless supply of impoverished women knocking on doors and offering cheap labor, it was difficult to find anyone who didn't already have servants.

In desperation, I visited Sister Veronica, the nun who ran the sewing classes for teenage girls, to ask if the sisters could use an extra cook or cleaning woman around the convent or the private school that they ran. When Sister Veronica met with me in the abbey's guest parlor, she offered me cookies and tea on a tray. She was peaceful as usual, radiating a warm, steady joy despite her precarious health and her obvious sorrow over the recent death of her small dog. She had been in and out of the hospital and seemed to have accepted the fact that death could come for her any day.

Even with a ceiling fan whirring overhead, the room was stuffy and hot, and I felt sweaty and impatient with her small talk. When I told her about Meena's unemployment dilemma, she told me that there were no openings at the school or the convent and there was nothing she could do to help Meena. I was jarred by the finality of her reply, and I began to cry as I expressed my sense of urgency and despair.

"Be tough-minded and tender-hearted," Sister Caris told me gently. "Don't let things get to you and break you down." She looked at me with the eyes of a compassionate grandmother. "You're young and you're still in a strange country—do what you can do, but what you can't do, leave to God. You can't save the world."

"I know," I said, but I didn't know. The sister's equanimity made me angry. What had seemed like wisdom before now struck me as anesthetizing platitudes. I didn't stay much longer, and I left feeling tired, yet already planning my next move.

* * *

Wracking my brain for any possible solution, I decided to phone Bebi, an Indian woman who lived in another slum and worked for a Muslim NGO. I knew her through my teammates, who lived nearby her in that community. A self-styled social worker, Bebi had grown up in the slum herself and had never gone to school, but she had gained informal experience through a government aid program which had hired her to help implement a development project in her neighborhood several years ago. Bebi still lived in poverty herself, but she had told me several weeks before that she could find a place for Meena to work and live with her kids if she went through with her divorce. I explained the new situation to her—which had the same sharp edges of desperation as the old situation—and she confidently told me to bring Meena to meet her, and she would connect her with the job.

Yet instead of meeting us herself, Bebi sent her sister-in-law to escort Meena, her four-year-old daughter Guria, and me to meet with the potential employer. Bebi's sister-in-law led us to an inconspicuous looking gate in a wall, where she talked with a guard. Another servant was summoned and came out to stare at us.

"You're going to introduce us to the ma'am?" I asked.

She nodded, looking a bit dazed.

"I told her that the family likes cleanliness," the sister-in-law told her, "That they want their servants to be clean and pure, too, and she should bathe before she comes."

The woman still didn't talk or move. Meena wasn't dirty, but her clothes were old, and her skin was very dark. Her teeth were stained from chewing *paan*, the mixture of areca nut and tobacco rolled in betel leaf that was so ubiquitous among rural and working-class Indians, and she had an abrasive, village way of speaking. But Guria was dirty, since it was impossible to keep small children clean when they played all day on the dirt alleyways and floors of the slum, especially when they didn't have enough clothes to change every day.

"So, shall we go?" I pressed.

Reluctantly, the servant took us through the gate and into a wide, paved road lined with six or seven of the biggest houses I had ever seen in the city. An extremely light-skinned boy played in the road while his light-skinned mother looked on from just inside her own massive gate. She eyed us with a mixture of curiosity and suspicion.

"The family holds about four *milaads* out here every year," Bebi's sister-in-law said with a sweep of her hand as we walked through a decorative metal gate and into a marble courtyard lined with potted plants. "They always give out food and sweets to all the servants at those times," she told Meena.

Meena was looking around expectantly, squinting her eyes in the contrast of this new hope amongst the shadows.

The woman of the house looked at us through the screen door, then disappeared again into the house. We took off our shoes and climbed the half-flight of stairs to the main floor. It was dimly lit inside. The floor was marble there, too. We padded across the cool stone to the edge of a large living room and stood next to the wrought-iron banister of an elaborate staircase leading to the second floor.

The ma'am, seated on a large sofa, listened cautiously to Meena's introduction. It was clear to me from the sister-in-law's words that there had been no advance notice of or planning for this visit. After a moment, the ma'am's curious eyes rested on me. I introduced myself, and as soon as she had confirmed that I was a foreigner, she invited me to sit on the large, comfortable sofa opposite her. Not wanting to cause any unproductive offense, I accepted.

Meena, the sister-in-law, and the other house servants squatted on the floor against the wall, and Guria played on the marble tiles in front of them while Meena told the ma'am about her husband's sudden death, her lost job, and the hungry children in her house. I didn't like the dynamic. My white skin and my English had automatically put me into the Important People category. I looked down uncomfortably at the People Who Sit on the Floor. The ma'am also regarded them uncomfortably. To be specific, she regarded *Meena* uncomfortably.

"I don't think she'll be able to do the kind of work that I need," she said at last. "I already have someone to do the dishes and the floors. I need someone to make the beds and to take out linens and put them away in the wardrobes. Also, she would need to be able to run a microwave. I don't think she'll be able to do that." She was speaking to me in English.

"I don't think it's that difficult to run a microwave," I said, smiling reassuringly. "She can learn."

"No, I need someone who's had experience doing these kinds of things before," she said, glancing back at Meena with a furrowed brow. "Otherwise there will be problems in the house."

It was only later that it would strike me with complete clarity. What she was really saying was, "I care more about being inconvenienced by having my bed made the wrong way than I care about whether or not this family starves." In the moment, the only thing I felt was my body sinking into the couch, and the only thought looping through my head again and again was, *This isn't going to work. Now what?*

When Meena realized that the new start that had been promised to her did not actually exist, she started crying. "I have no one to help me, no one!" she lamented to the women sitting next to her on the floor. "What will I do?"

"They're really worried about food at her house," I tried again with the ma'am. "They haven't been eating."

"Oh, we can help with that," she said. She got up and went into another room—to get some food, I imagined— and I took advantage of the opportunity to slip down to the floor with the others. The sister-in-law and the other servant protested, but I told them I felt strange sitting up there alone on the couch. They laughed at my quirk, but accepted it.

When the ma'am came back, she had a notepad and a pen in her hand. She took down my number, promising to call if she ever needed someone to do the kind of work Meena was looking for. As we all stood to leave, she told Meena with a decency that mocked sincerity, "If you ever need anything, you can come back here again."

When would she ever need "anything" more than she did at that moment? I wondered. She was out of work and hadn't eaten all day. If the woman was too tight-fisted to spare even a *roti* or a piece of fruit right then, what kind of divine intervention would be needed to spontaneously create generosity in her heart a few days or weeks later?

"Come back during Ramazan," Bebi's sister-in-law said consolingly as we walked back across the marble court-yard. "They always give out food to people during that time." As though the promise of a good meal four months away could lift a hungry woman's spirits.

Back in the slum, Meena and Guria came over to my house. I served chai as we all sat silently on the floor, dull and deflated. I offered them leftover *daliya kichari* from lunch, a nutritious mixture of lentils and cracked wheat, but they didn't want it because they both had colds, and Meena was convinced that cracked wheat would make the illness worse. They turned down fresh bananas for the same reason. Indian culture has complex categories of which foods are "hot" or "cold," and cold foods should be avoided by people who are sick. I felt exhausted by the myriad obstacles that were keeping my neighbor from getting back on her feet, not least of all those she routinely imposed on herself because of her religion and culture.

This failure to land a job for Meena or even to feed her hungry daughter a banana piled on top of a long series of frustrated attempts to help. Andy and I had repeatedly invited her to come over for dinner at our house, but she always refused, insisting that if she was seen publicly accepting help from us, then everyone else would stop helping her, since they would assume that we were giving her everything she needed. The only thing she really wanted from us was cash, but that was exactly the kind of long-term patron-client relationship that we wanted to avoid.

* * *

Between visits with Meena and her daughters, I continued to spend bewildering hours with Zahera, whose mother's illness had intensified to the point that Zahera spent all of her waking hours caring for her.

At night, exhausted by my day's visits, I listened through the wall to my next-door neighbor screaming at her children. One sweltering afternoon, I stood in our doorway watching neighbors hold back a violent, intoxicated man from physically attacking his wife in the alley in front of our house. Early one morning, I wandered from room to room in an overcrowded hospital, trying to help my pregnant neighbor get an ultrasound, basic blood tests, and essential prenatal vitamins and nutritional supplements. Another day, I visited a neighbor who had been admitted to a private clinic several days before for symptoms of high blood pressure. After disputing the huge medical bill with the doctor and his staff, forcing them to take me through the invoice line by line, I discovered that she had been charged exorbitant amounts of money for a series of IV drips filled with saline and antibiotics to treat cold symptoms. Nothing had been done to address her blood pressure.

I raged against the inflexible, ineffective systems which prevented the poor from accessing basic healthcare and exploited their vulnerability by overcharging for unnecessary or fake care. I grieved the suffering around me. And I despaired at my inability to solve any of these problems. What could my small effort accomplish in the face of thousands of years of social convention, generational dysfunction, and structural injustice?

I had moved into the slum with dreams of changing people's lives. I had thought that incarnational living was as simple to do as it was to explain. I had imagined that concerned friends who were willing to journey alongside people could lift them out of poverty. Yet Meena's predicament was teaching me that the transformation I sought would require far more patience and time than I had anticipated.

* * *

Just before returning to India, I had relished my enlightening conversation with God, which had given me the courage to continue living in the slum. Yet back in the trenches just a few months later, I was still struggling to integrate the new perspective I had gained into my everyday life. I kept circling back to the same old fears and false beliefs again and again.

Eventually, my anxiety and fear of others' expectations nearly paralyzed me, sometimes keeping me from leaving my room. I would wake feeling discouraged and reluctant to leave the peace and comfort of my bed in order to face the day. My days were so unpredictable that I knew I could not expect to feel that peace, comfort, and solitary quiet again until I lay down at night to sleep. Whenever I did venture out, I felt an utter loss of control as I opened myself to whatever conversations or crises might arise. Most of the people we knew in the slum had been abused as children, and though this explained the shocking emotional ignorance that I often observed in people's interactions with one another, it was heart-wrenching to see neglect, abuse, and humiliation meted out to some of the most vulnerable people in the community.

I wondered why I didn't feel close to God as I lived among the poor. I wondered why I was unable to find joy in serving others if this was the path Jesus had given me to walk. Though I felt God's presence and frequently caught glimpses of beauty and joy, those encounters were not enough to tip the balance away from all the ugliness I saw and the stress and discouragement that I felt. For nearly as long as we had lived in the slum, I had struggled under the pressure to be or do or give what people needed in one unpredictable crisis after another. Now I had reached the point of feeling that I didn't have what it would take to be the kind of friend that I had set out to be for my neighbors.

* * *

Spring 2014

In my fruitless search to find work for Meena that would secure the wellbeing of her family, I began to lose track of the plot line. I had gotten sidetracked from my original, humble goal of suffering alongside the poor and had begun to measure the value of my time based on the effectiveness of my interventions. From there, it was a short road to despair, because bad things kept happening to Meena and her family with no resolution and no catharsis—just one banal disappointment after another, dripping out like water from a leaky faucet.

During the time I was growing up in the States, most of the people around me usually seemed to be doing well, and most of the stories I heard seemed to turn out well in the end—so it had been easy for me to believe in the victory of the cross and the promise of new life. Yet it was much harder for me to keep faith in the resurrection in my new little corner of the world, since most of the people in our slum were not doing OK. As I witnessed them doing horrible things to each other and having horrible things done to them, it became painfully obvious that their suffering wasn't going to be completely done away with anytime soon.

As we journeyed through Lent, I found myself meditating on the silent Saturday after the crucifixion, when Jesus remained in the tomb. And a few days before Easter, I found myself navigating the thin place that stretches between hope and despair, uncertain whether or not anything we did was worth it, doubting if all would be made well in the end. As I contemplated Jesus' tragic death and the way that His closest friends betrayed and abandoned him, and as I heard His anguished voice wondering aloud from the cross whether God was still with Him in the midst of so much pain, I realized with startling clarity that the resurrection was a surprise.

Everyone, *everyone,* had given up on Jesus—even His closest friends and followers, whom He had spent years teaching and preparing for that moment. He had told them so many times that He would suffer and die, but that it wouldn't be the end. And when He was tortured and killed by the state and the religious institution, they fumbled around in the dark, wondering what the Kingdom had meant and how their fearless leader had failed to accomplish His mission. He was dead and gone, and they thought it was over. The women mourned Him and prepared spices to pay their last respects; the men returned to their fishing nets, disillusioned.

Had they not experienced such miserable despair, perhaps they would not have felt such profuse joy when they discovered Jesus alive. Their tangible experience of moving through death and loss to new life strengthened their faith from that point onward. If they had confidently expected His triumphant return all along, they wouldn't have known what it meant to be delivered from danger or pain. Real suffering brings questions to the surface—even to the lips of Jesus: "My God, my God, why have you forsaken me?"[10]

---

[10] Matthew 27:46

So Jesus didn't hold his friends' doubt against them—not even Peter, who denied his best friend and teacher three times to save his own skin. Instead, Jesus cooked him breakfast on the beach, reinstated him, and entrusted him with the future of his movement ("on this rock I will build my church. . ."[11]). Peter experienced resurrection in his own heart when Jesus forgave him, and he also learned to trust himself again. Later, this former turncoat proved himself faithful to the point of death on a cross himself.

In my day-to-day life in the slum, I often felt overwhelmed by the state of the world, and I wondered how the Kingdom could ever come. I found it hard to imagine history somehow rolling on from the present into heaven on earth. But as I read this story, I realized that there was a place within the Easter narrative for the grief and confusion I so frequently felt. For Peter and the others, there was as little continuity between their experience of absolute loss on Friday and absolute joy on Sunday as there was between my current experience of the impoverished, suffering world as it was and the world as it will be when it is fully restored.

That story reminded me that I was not lost. I was seeing Saturday. But Sunday morning would come—just when I least expected it.

And glimpses of resurrection joy did come in little signs of hope, tiny as mustard seeds, which sprung up through the ground of despair. We saw resurrection in our relationships when we offered and received forgiveness over a conflict with our former landlady, Gita, or when we creatively imagined new possibilities out of apparent failures within our team. We caught a glimpse of the Kingdom when Amna cooked meals for us while I was recovering from a minor surgery and couldn't get out of bed. We were a surrogate family made up of different lan-

---

[11] Matthew 16:18

guages, cultures, and religions, choosing to build community instead of walls. There was resurrection in my own heart when old wounds were bandaged and began to heal.

There was hope when we would sow and sow and sow, and then one seed (maybe one in a hundred) would burst into life. I saw one of those tender shoots when our landlady, Yazmin, began coming over almost every day for literacy lessons, determinedly resurrecting her childhood dream of learning to read after decades of hope deferred. Another sprouting seed came when a man in the neighborhood reported that he had been pleasantly surprised by the positive outcome when he had taken Andy's advice to talk through a conflict with his wife instead of beating her. I knew that these tender shoots were small and fragile, and I had no idea if they would ever be able to thrive in the soil of our slum, but they were still signs of hope, glimmers of new life, and I was grateful.

* * *

Then, several long months after Iqbal's funeral, Meena found a job as a domestic servant, working for a wage similar to what she had previously been earning. Though we were happy to hear about her new employment, Meena's new job had nothing to do with any of the jobs that Andy or I had sought out, nor any of the plans we had tried to put in motion.

I tried to content myself with the knowledge that the friendship, emotional support, and occasional material relief that Andy and I had offered to Meena and her daughters had been meaningful during that dark season following Iqbal's death. Yet our involvement had made little to no difference in their circumstances, and they were continuing now in much the same way they had before the funeral—minus the abuse, which had also been ended by natural causes rather than through our intervention. We felt haunted by our inability to make a significant difference in our neighbors' lives. The complex layers of personal baggage, unjust systems, environmental factors, cultural priorities, and expectations continued to surprise, grieve, and anger me. I had also discovered that I was far more complex than I had realized before moving to India, and as I continued to journey through the painful process of learning how to respect my own limitations and needs, I felt more and more emotionally exhausted.

* * *

In the midst of these despairing feelings, I remembered a simple quotation from Mother Teresa that I had first read as a college student years before: "We can do no great things; only small things with great love." I also thought of Sister Veronica's words, which I had been too deafened by my fear of failure to hear at the time: "What you can't do, leave to God. You can't save the world."

I realized that I needed to recover the spirituality that Mother Theresa had first inspired in me: doing small things with great love instead driving to achieve visible, quantifiable, large-scale, structural change. Though I would love to see those things happen (and God knows they need to happen), I needed to remember that I was not a failure if they didn't happen—and I couldn't measure my effectiveness in terms of visible results. I was a very limited human being, and I could only have a limited impact on a limited number of people. That humbling revelation had been slowly unfolding within me over the past year, but it was already known to Jesus when He compared the Kingdom to yeast subtly and slowly working through the dough. Notice He mentioned nothing about fireworks, mass revolution, or impressive charts and statistics.

I was settling into the realization that what was most important for my neighbors in the slum was that I was with them. Though I was unable to solve their problems, I could be a witness, an advocate, and a friend, willing to walk alongside them as they suffered the frustration of powerless grief in the midst of their struggles. I could carry their sacred stories and help them to recognize that sacredness for themselves.

Day after day, my work was to be present to the people around me—I might feed someone, help someone get medical care, get someone's kids into school, or persuade someone to stop using violence on others. And by faithfully tending those things over time, I might someday get the chance to be part of overturning unjust laws or actually fixing some of the broken structures that made life so difficult for the people around me. But ultimately, I was there to be with people rather than to fix them or to change their lives, and I wanted to have the perseverance to continue being with them and taking joy in being with them, whether or not they or their circumstances ever changed.

I was also discovering that this ministry of presence mirrored God's own presence with me. God was not present merely to fix me or help me, but because She loved me and took delight in being with me. Some days I would think, "Sure, you were with me today, God, but what good did it do?" But most days, I was just glad for the consolation of Her presence, for the peace of experiencing Her ongoing love and acceptance—even when I disappointed myself and felt useless or destructive.

11
LIVING IN LOVE'S EMBRACE

Spring 2014

"Why does Jesus say I thirst? What does it mean? Something so hard to explain in words. . . I thirst is something much deeper than Jesus just saying, 'I love you.' Until you know deep inside that Jesus thirsts for you — you can't begin to know who He wants to be for you. Or who He wants you to be for Him."

—Mother Teresa

When I first read about Mother Teresa's life while I was in college, I was confused about why she spent her first fifteen years in India teaching the daughters of Calcutta's elite at a posh private school. *Why did she waste all that time before starting her life's work with the destitute and dying?* I wondered.

But as I lived through the experience of burning out in India, it dawned on me that those years had not been wasted. She would have been living as a nun that whole time, spending hours in prayer and contemplation every day, getting to know Jesus intimately, and anchoring herself in His Love. This hard-won intimacy with Jesus, slowly and lovingly woven through years of shared life, had allowed her to recognize Jesus in the first destitute woman she rescued from the street and in every beggar and child she encountered after that. She recognized Jesus in His distressing disguises, because she already knew Jesus. She had spent a lifetime with Him. The experience of being loved by Christ rooted her work in joyful, compassionate instinct rather than duty.

My journey up to this point had been from the opposite direction. Like peeling back the layers of an onion, I had begun from what was outwardly visible. I had spent my teenage years and early twenties asking myself how Jesus had lived. And since Jesus had hung out with the poor, the blind, the sick, and the outcasts, as well as enemy soldiers, their yellow-bellied tax collector cronies, and heretical "half-breeds" like the Samaritans, I figured that I would do likewise. I'd find the poor and the outcasts, befriend them, tell them that God loves them, and invite them into the community of the Kingdom, where there is always room at the table. I eagerly and energetically followed my Teacher with all of my heart, soul, mind, and strength, expending energy, making sacrifices, and living as radically as I could. As I sought to act on what I read about Jesus' life in the gospels by reaching out to others, I was drawn into a deeper experience of God. Thus my external actions and circumstances shaped my internal transformation.

But as I grew more exhausted by our life in the slum, and as I came face-to-face with my own limitations, I began to wonder if all the external change in my life had outpaced my internal growth. Somewhere along the way, I had mistaken the means for the end. My ultimate goal had become to serve the poor by living as simply as possible in the worst possible place and doing as much as possible to help. Yet I was discovering that compassion, service, and simplicity were not ends in themselves, but were means of communing with God, recognizing God in myself and the people around me, and joyfully living in Love's embrace.

Only in the throes of repeatedly overextending myself to respond to bottomless needs did I stumble into questions such as: *How did Jesus sustain this life? What was making Him tick from the inside?* Following my Teacher as far as possible on my own steam had brought me to the limits of myself. I needed an inner connection, an internal fire that could transform the difficult life of discipleship into the easy yoke and the light burden that Jesus describes in Matthew 11 (verses 28–30). I even began to wonder if I might have done better to spend fifteen years in a monastery before trying to live in a slum. Instead, I had sallied out into the darkest corners of the world, seeking to share a flame that I had barely begun to kindle within myself. How could I share Living Water from a well that so often seemed to be drying up within my own heart?

When Andy and I first arrived in India for our site visit, we had spent a few days volunteering at Mother Teresa's house for the destitute and dying. I had wanted to be near the love—to absorb it perhaps, from proximity. But while the sisters laughed, joked, and prayed the rosary aloud, I struggled to find Jesus in the midst of my disgust and fear. I get nauseous around blood, and there were plenty of open wounds and rotting flesh to test the strength of my stomach and my mind.

As the sisters went about their duties, I didn't observe any outward clues about how they survived—or rather, thrived—surrounded by the broken bodies of patients who would never be made well. But it dawned on me that the key to their joyful lives was what they did in secret: the mass celebrated just after dawn each day, the quiet hours of prayer in the evening, the slow-growing courtship with Jesus that made their hearts strong and contented with love and lifted the veil from their eyes to see their Beloved in the faces of the suffering people who came to them. Yet in my ongoing life in the slum, I struggled to recognize Christ's crucified eyes in the downcast gaze of a drug-addicted abusive husband, a bitter mother-in-law, or a self-satisfied official, who maintained his potbelly with mercenary calculations of human misery minus power equals profit.

I was learning the hard way that this secret life with God could not be bypassed. Suffering, patience, and hard work could not be truncated or avoided—and the fruits of such a life could not be imitated. I was well-versed in the evils, suffering, and despair of the world. I had felt power-less, frustrated, angry, and disillusioned as I watched my poor neighbors get ground down by systems of domination with no hope in sight. But I had not yet persevered in the hope of things unseen. I barely recognized the faint, reassuring whisper of the Friend within me. I didn't have the assurance that everything would be alright, simply be-cause She was there.

For all my energy, effort, service, and courage, for all my idealism, theologizing, and spoken admiration of Je-sus, for all my passion and righteous indignation over the injustices of this world, I realized that I was still a begin-ner in that inner life. What I had failed to realize until I was smack-dab in the middle of the needy crowds, trying to offer hope to the down-and-out people who had been spit out by the system, was that Jesus didn't launch or sus-tain his mission with grandiose principles or the sheer force of willpower. I had neglected to pay attention to the thirty years of preparation that led up to Jesus' public life. I had rushed past the forty days of fasting and prayer in the desert that immediately preceded His ministry. And I had skipped over the lonely hours of prayer and solitude that sustained Him.

Jesus knew that He could not survive if His strength was not constantly renewed by God's presence within Him. He knew that He could not maintain hope amidst the misery that surrounded Him if He did not nurture an intense awareness of God's loving and abiding presence. He knew that He could not experience joy in the midst of exhaustion and suffering if He did not seek intimacy with that Presence in all circumstances. He knew that He could not weather frequent rejection and confrontation—and eventually total betrayal—if He did not cultivate an unshakeable sense of His identity as the Beloved of God. The awareness of God's loving presence in all circumstances made Him entirely free from the opinions of others—free enough to serve people without needing their gratitude, and free to extend love even to those who repaid His compassion with hatred. Jesus received the gift of this unflinching love and courage because He had experienced God's unconditional love in the depths of His own being. That love defined Him, and it became the root of everything He did.

Yet I had tried to embark on the messy occupation of loving broken, wounded people in a context of grinding poverty without sufficient preparation, testing, or sustenance. I had desperately tried to build an identity for myself out of all the good things I was doing: *See how much I suffer! See how much I am willing to sacrifice!* my soul yelled. *I will earn your love yet.* And so my labor of love had become exhausting, and my feverish attempts to pour myself out had revealed an inner emptiness that I had never noticed before. I ached to be filled with the unconditional love of God within the expanse of my inner being. I longed to claim my identity as the Beloved.

I now knew that God was not waiting for me to display faithful obedience, courage, or self-denial in order to embrace me. I knew that She was embracing me even then—with my empty hands and tattered clothes—as the beggar that I was. As the child who could never do anything to make her Parent love her more or less. As a prodigal daughter returned home after all my fruitless attempts at making a life worth living for myself apart from Her love.

During those dark days, I read Henri Nouwen's *Home Tonight: Further Reflections on the Parable of the Prodigal Son,* and I recognized myself in the dutiful but miserable older brother as well as in the prodigal himself. I also recognized myself in the desperate people who surrounded me in the slum—people for whose pain I knew God's heart was breaking every day. I thought, *I am the poor, I am the sick, I am the rejected.* I waited in grief and hope for the mercy of God to reveal my true identity to me, for God to rock me to sleep in strong arms like a newborn baby, safe and wanted and loved. My neighbors often bore their scars and their struggles openly on their faces and in the rough edges of their lives, but mine were hidden deep inside.

I am the poor, and they are me. God is in us, and we are in Her. I was beginning to see that perhaps the whole purpose of life was for us to realize, together, the depth of our poverty and to help one another to accept the Love that would satisfy our deepest need.

III.
FAILURE AND GRACE

May–September 2014

"The first call is frequently to follow Jesus or to prepare ourselves to do wonderful or noble things for the Kingdom. We are appreciated and admired by family, by friends, or by the community. The second call comes later, when we accept that we cannot do big and heroic things for Jesus; it is a time of renunciation, humiliation, and humility."

—Jean Vanier

12
INSIDER ON THE OUTSIDE,
OUTSIDER ON THE INSIDE

May 2014

Shortly after Easter, Michael, Kat, and their two sons left for a year's sabbatical in Australia, shrinking the supportive community of our team by half. Attempting to fill the relational void their absence carved out within me, I began making more of an effort to connect with other foreigners in the city—people who did not share our vision of living in intentional poverty, but who could relate to the experience of living in India as an outsider, and understand the life I had left behind. Even as I felt emotionally and psychologically drained by the demands of friendship with my neighbors, I continued to long for the kind of life-giving, supportive connections with others that could help to sustain me in the slum.

Later that spring, I met up with a Canadian friend for coffee, across town in Ilahabad's upscale shopping district. Andy came to meet me afterward, and we wandered around, enjoying the spacious sidewalks as we passed huge, glass storefronts filled with mannequins sporting both Western designer ensembles and luxurious saris worth hundreds of dollars.

We passed the flashy mall a neighbor had described as "cool in the summer and warm in the winter," where she and her family had gone to watch the "moving staircases," but had been too terrified to ride them from one floor to another. I imagined the people milling around us, wearing Western clothes and carrying smartphones, were not impressed by—let alone afraid of—the escalators inside. Inside the mall, brightly lit signs for KFC and Dominos Pizza welcomed patrons into upscale restaurants that bore no resemblance to the fast-food joints where our family had stopped on the long road trips of my youth.

After two years of living in slums, Andy and I were still struggling to bridge the chasm between the affluent, Western world we had come from and the impoverished, cross-cultural context in which we now lived. As we explored this new part of Ilahabad, we felt as if we had crossed back into our old lives—and yet geographically we were still in the same city where our neighbors struggled to survive from one day to the next.

Back in America, I had worn Western clothes, carried an iPhone, driven a car, and gone to restaurants and malls with friends—as the people milling around me were doing now. Yet in all my time in India, I had never shopped at a mall like the huge one we had just passed. I had traveled all over Ilahabad without ever seeing these coffee shops, stores, bars, and restaurants filled with wealthy—and presumably educated—Indians. But I had been to village weddings and Muslim saints' graves, outdoor markets and public hospitals, train stations and slums. In America, I would have gone out for gelato to celebrate something important. But in India, I marked special occasions by eating buffalo biryani with my neighbors at home.

As Andy and I walked past places we would have frequented in America, but which seemed jarring and disorienting in the middle of Ilahabad, I struggled to know my place in the world. I was a foreigner living in India with a laptop, an iPod, a Facebook account, and access to nearly limitless resources and opportunity. Yet I lived without AC, spoke Hindi, wore bangles on my wrists instead of a watch and loose-fitting *salwar kameez* suits instead of jeans, and spent most of my time with village migrants who lived below the poverty line.

The middle-class Indians and Westerners I knew who worked for NGOs wore jeans, kept up with one another on social media, and were familiar with the city's nightlife. But I had joined a community in which women scarcely left the house without their heads covered and where jeans would have been interpreted as a mark of Western culture and wealth—or even as an indication of loose morals and a cry for inappropriate attention. My Western friends talked about where they shopped to find imported brands, peanut butter, organic products, and even bacon. But my neighbors could only afford to buy the conventionally grown vegetables at the local market, and I couldn't even remember the last time I had eaten pork, since Andy and I had given it up after moving into our Muslim neighborhood. *An insider on the outside. An outsider on the inside.* By outward appearances, we had begun to look like we belonged, yet inwardly, our Western sensibilities and ways of thinking remained. We could never be exactly like our neighbors.

I reminded myself that we had decided to live in the slum because we had wanted to learn how to relate to people who were different from us by meeting them on their own turf. But here in this wealthy area, the people who resembled my Indian friends and neighbors—whom others saw as lower-class and "backward"—were catering to the rich as rickshaw pullers and child balloon sellers, or they were the beggars standing on the side of the road, entreating passing shoppers for change. Where did I fit in? Was I a wealthy shopper, unaware and uninvolved? Or was I standing with the poor on the sidelines? These questions haunted me, and I had to ask myself if we were just putting on some kind of act, pretending to be poor.

But as I held this question, I saw the faces of my neighbors. And I remembered how often I had told them that they were experts at the things I wanted to learn. They knew the ins and outs of living in the slum. They knew all about Islam, Hindi, and Indian cooking. They understood instinctively the complicated family trees that made up the community and the nuanced customs that governed each of the relationships within them. They had weathered grief and difficulty with creativity and resilience. They had learned how to live with few possessions. They knew how to give generously, because they had so little that any sharing was necessarily sacrificial. They knew what it meant to trust in God, because they could not trust in stocks, savings, influential contacts, or a strong resume to protect them and provide for their future. They knew what it meant to depend on God, because there was no earthly security or comfort to distract them from the stark reality that they were often powerless before forces that were far beyond their control—whereas my relative wealth often blinded me to the fact that, ultimately, I shared this universal human predicament. As I thought of everything I had learned about myself and my place in the world from my neighbors, I knew that I was not pretending to be someone else. Even though my choices might seem strange to others, I knew that the essential core of who I was remained unchanged.

After our walk through that cosmopolitan shopping district, Andy and I returned to our community. As we walked back over the drainage canal and headed down the steep slope leading from the main road into the slum, it felt as if we had crossed into a completely different world. We passed a shack near the entrance to the neighborhood and waved to the malnourished family who lived there, the family with the stunted children that played in the alley and the skinny baby that the mother held on her hip whenever she stood in the doorway. The little world of our neighborhood seemed more real than upscale Ilahabad— or our world in America, for that matter. No climate control to shelter us from the elements. No trash collection service to disguise how much waste we were actually generating. No separation from the poverty in which the majority of the world's population lives. As challenging as it was for Andy and me to adjust to our life in the slums of India, we knew those realities were more representative of the human experience than the comforts of our home country. *An insider on the outside. An outsider on the inside.*

* * *

For the next several months, Andy and I agonized about whether we should stay on in the slum, or if it was time to leave. We had come to India with the intention of staying for the rest of our lives, yet as we journeyed into the heat of the summer, it became increasingly apparent that I would not be able to emotionally and psychologically withstand our current circumstances much longer. One night, just as Andy and I were preparing to go to bed, acrid smoke began pouring in through the window, which we had left open to provide some ventilation in the stifling heat of the humid, monsoon nights. This wasn't the first time that toxic fumes had inundated our room, and I went from calm to furious in the space of a few seconds as we coughed and struggled to breathe. We both knew that our neighbor was burning the protective coating off of electrical wires in the courtyard below, so that he could sell the wires themselves as scrap metal.

"Kafeel!" I called out the window. "We can't breathe up here!"

"What?" our neighbor called back from below.

"Stop burning plastic!" I yelled, making no effort to hide the anger in my voice. "We can't breathe because of the smoke!"

"It won't take long!" he called back. "Just a little while longer!"

I was livid.

"It's OK," Andy said, trying to calm me down. "Just relax."

"No! This is ridiculous," I shot back, hurriedly changing back into my daytime clothes and heading out the door. I moved with determination down the alley toward Kafeel's door. "Kafeel!" I called out, pounding on his wooden door.

Kafeel's wife came to the door and cracked it open. "I've told him to put the fire out, but he's drunk," she said apologetically. "It won't be much longer. Maybe half an hour."

If I hadn't been physically and mentally exhausted, I might have recognized the expression on her face as fear.

"Kafeel!" I yelled out again. "Put that fire out! It's late at night and we are trying to sleep, but our whole house is full of smoke!" I could hear him laughing and talking with other men inside the courtyard.

"He's drunk. Please," she implored, "don't make him angry. It will only be a few more minutes."

The realization dawned on me that she would be the one to pay the price if I pushed any further. Exasperated, I turned and walked away. In the morning, I replayed the events of the previous evening in my mind and felt ashamed of having lost my temper and endangered both myself and my neighbor by provoking her intoxicated husband. Yet in the moment, I had acted on instinct rather than reason, and I wasn't sure I would be able to respond differently if I found myself in similar circumstances in the future. This sobering admission worried me.

A week later, Andy and I were sitting inside our room when we heard a man yelling in the alley below. Looking down from the roof where our laundry was hung up to dry, we saw a neighbor beating his wife in front of our house, and we rushed downstairs to intervene. By the time we reached the ground floor doorway, the woman was lying on the ground in the fetal position while her husband kicked her. We moved swiftly to get between them, Andy holding the man back and me standing in front of the woman to shield her. My adrenaline was high and my heart was pounding in my chest. When the man lunged toward me, trying to break free of Andy, I felt the impulse to punch him. Shaken, I stepped away.

By then, other neighbors had gotten involved, and they were restraining the man and crouching around his injured wife. My mind was stretched thin and taut as I wondered what I would have done if I had remained standing in front of the man instead of walking away. *Would I have physically attacked my neighbor?* I asked myself. As my neighbors continued to shout over one another, I leaned against the doorway, feeling my heart thudding in my chest, and hearing the thought beating steadily in my mind: *you have lost control.*

By July, we recognized our urgent need to decide our future, and so we spent two weeks away from the slum in order to get some rest, get out of survival mode, and find the perspective we needed to discern the way forward. Halfway across the country in Darjeeling, Andy and I began to discuss abandoning our life plan of living forever among the poor in the slums of India. We moved slowly through our days in Darjeeling, leaving our hotel for little else besides hot bowls of Tibetan noodles and cups of coffee at quiet cafés, where we spent hours reading and journaling. Back in our small room, I sat on the bed in silence, stretching out visions of the future before me, weighing the possibilities. I thought about the freedom God had given me to return to India or to choose another path. I had returned to India hoping to make our life there work, but I knew it wasn't working.

As Andy and I talked, we stood on a rooftop garden overlooking the snowcapped Himalayas and the small villages nestled into the slopes of the verdant valleys below. I took in the expanse of the sky and the fresh, cool breeze blowing across my face. Staring at the mountains and the potted flowers that surrounded me on the roof, I felt like a climber summiting one of those icy peaks in the distance: straining my lungs in the thin air; hungry for oxygen and unable to get enough of it. I wanted to hold tightly to the tranquil beauty around me and never let it go.

But my thoughts inexorably returned to the hot, crowded city we had left behind for this retreat. I pictured the narrow, dusty alleyways of our neighborhood; the black, sludgy drainage canal; and the squalid shacks that hugged the shore. I heard the angry voices through thin walls, the blows falling on innocent women and children, and the endless pleading of my neighbors in one crisis after another. I felt suffocated, desperate to escape the crushing weight of responsibility I felt for so many people in Ilahabad, whose chaotic lives had become enmeshed in my own.

"I don't want to live there anymore," I told Andy, bursting into tears. As the words washed over me, I felt immense relief.

During the remaining days of our retreat, we talked about leaving Ilahabad. In giving up our life in India, we knew that we were also relinquishing our self-made identity as strong, compassionate People Who Help, and it was painful to imagine letting go of the work that had come to define us.

Though my deteriorating mental health and my decreased ability to function amidst the stress of slum life was pushing us toward leaving, as I quieted my heart to listen, I began to understand that our departure did not need to be a fear-driven retreat from anything—a failure or a rescue operation. Rather than anxiously scrambling toward any possible means of escape, I began to hear a calm, hopeful voice assuring me that we could intentionally turn toward something else. As my sense of panic subsided, Andy and I both felt deeper clarity that God was inviting us into a season of rest.

We realized that if we continued to prop up our self-made identities, we wouldn't be able to receive the unconditional love of God, because our focus would remain on what we did or what other people thought of us. By the time we boarded the train to return to Ilahabad, our decision to leave had solidified—not as a renunciation of the ideals that had led us to live among the poor, but as a humble recognition that we needed deeper healing before we could live well the kind of life we believed in.

As I had encountered God in the distressing disguise of suffering humanity, I had been drawn into deeper love for myself and the people around me. I had been led beyond the limits of my competency and intellect into mystery, humble self-knowledge, and a hunger to cultivate the light of God within my heart more and more. I had also learned that I couldn't embody love for others before I experienced that love myself. I had come to India to seek God among the poor, and I had found Her there. But to my surprise, I had also found Her lodged deep within me. She hadn't been waiting for me to come to India to tell me that She approved of me. She had been delighting in me all along.

* * *

August 2014

India, my home for two and a half years, got under my skin and became part of me forever. India changed me irrevocably—expanding my capacity for love and pain, opening my eyes to suffering and joy. India also wore me thin, exhausted me, and brought me to the end of myself. Preparing to leave was both a significant relief and a significant loss.

As our departure drew near, Andy and I began having conversations with our friends and neighbors about our impending move, and we all shed a lot of tears. Outings, or simply drinking chai in my friends' homes, took on new significance. Friends stopped by to borrow our rat trap and stayed to talk for an hour, or they dropped by to practice reading and stayed for the afternoon. We held each moment with gratitude, knowing it would be all we had.

I told Zahera about our decision to leave on a hot and humid afternoon as we lay facing one another on the cool floor of her room with our heads resting on comfortable pillows. As I told her about our impending departure, I began to cry, and at first she began to comfort me—but when she realized that I would be gone in a few weeks, she started to cry, too.

"You won't be here for my wedding," she cried. "I thought you would be here for my wedding." We had often talked about my coming to visit her in the village after she was married, about getting to hold her first baby.

"I've told you all of my *dil ki baat*—the matters of the heart," Zahera sobbed. "I thought that if my mom died, I would be okay because I had my older sister." Tears fell sideways across the bridge of her nose. "But if my older sister leaves, what will I do? God always takes away the good things in my life. Every good thing is taken away!"

I held her hand and cried with her. I cried for each of the losses she had experienced, one after another. I cried because soon, she would be moving to a village with a boy and a family she didn't know. I cried because I knew that my leaving would cause her more sorrow, because no one was responsible for her well-being, because she had no one to trust with her deepest hopes, fears, and struggles. I cried because I loved her, and I longed for her world to be different.

* * *

Toward the end of August, Andy and I traveled with Zahera to the Muslim shrine in the small village where her mom and sister had been living for the past eight months, hoping for a miracle. We took a three-wheeled taxi from our neighborhood to the major intersection a few kilometers away, where beat-up jeeps loaded passengers for longer journeys out to the nearest small town and beyond. We sat crowded four to a bench, facing four other passengers on the opposite side, with several more wedged into an improvised seat facing the hatchback door behind that. Zahera was traveling with lots of luggage—two canvas bags stuffed with a change of clothes, a pressure cooker, and several kilos of rice and flour. We were bringing rations to her mom and sister so that they could eat for the next several weeks, since they were without any other source of income or food at the *mazar*.

As we sped along the highway, the familiar city slowly gave way to newer developments—mostly high-end, gated, luxury apartment complexes, universities, and medical facilities. Then the scenery gradually turned to green rice fields and open space. In the next small town, we got into another crowded jeep to take us a few kilometers further before finally getting out and walking the last leg of the journey through a small village to our destination.

The village itself struck me as a charming enclave of classical old houses with carved wooden doorways and brickwork. There were hand pumps and ancient wells, monkeys and small children wandering around, big trees shading green spaces, and water buffalo wallowing in streams and standing around in fields. There was also a steady breeze, and the area was decidedly cooler than the crowded, paved city we had left behind.

"I thought it would be bad to live in a village," I said, knowing that Zahera's family had been searching for her future husband among their rural connections, "but now I see there are also advantages to living here. It's so beautiful and relaxed. So much space."

Zahera laughed sarcastically. "You think it's a lovely place, do you? And do you realize that there's also no electricity out here? I don't think it's a nice place at all."

Soon we came to a small cluster of vendors selling snacks and devotional paraphernalia on either side of a dirt path, which ended at a tall, white, plastered gate with painted green Arabic script and geometric designs arching across the top. The *mazar* lay just beyond this gate, but it wasn't visible from the footpath. A columned veranda with a tin roof fanned out to the left of the gate. The space between each of the pillars had been claimed by a different individual or family who was staying at the *mazar* to seek miraculous healing from the *baba* for some physical or psychological ailment. Sheets had been folded over clotheslines to create half-walls around each of the makeshift dwellings, offering some privacy. Beyond the veranda, green fields stretched away into the distance toward stands of palm trees on the horizon. The scene would have been quaint and idyllic if it weren't for the obvious squalor of these lodgings. Directly in front of the crowded veranda, we spotted Zahera's mother, lying on a rope bed.

As we approached, she cried out in a pitiful, strained voice, and tears streamed down her face. Zahera's sister,

Neha, emerged from behind an improvised curtain wall and began to sob hysterically about being beaten, but our repeated questions of "What happened?" yielded no further information. Suddenly Neha collapsed, and Andy managed to catch her just before she hit the ground. He carried her over to the rope bed, and as I tried to shift her into a comfortable position on the woven rope, I was alarmed by the sharp, boney protrusion of her hip in my hand. She was dotted all over with mosquito bites, her thin arms were covered with scratches, and her hair was unwashed and stiff.

As her mother and sister wailed hysterically, Zahera's concern shifted to frustration. Local villagers came over and explained that Neha had been beaten because she had started a fight with one of the women who lived nearby. "Who can deal with her?" one man said.

It pained me to hear Zahera yell at her sister to stop crying, her voice sharp with embarrassment and anger.

I tried to explain to the man who had criticized Neha that she only had the mind of a child and that she didn't understand what she was doing. I knew that making her afraid would only cause her more stress and make her behavior worse.

I hated repeating the derogatory language that people used to describe Neha—"*kam dimaag*" ("less brain") or "*bachche jese*" ("like a child")—but I didn't know any other way to explain her mental disability in Hindi, and I knew that the villagers had no framework for understanding it anyway. Nearby, another teenage girl with an obvious mental disability knelt limply in the dust, a vacant expression in her eyes and an absent-minded smile playing on her lips. One of the villagers told me that her family had been living at the *mazar* for two years, hoping that she would be healed.

After Zahera's mother and sister had calmed down, Andy and I spoke discreetly to Zahera. "They can't go on like this. Neha is going to go crazy if she stays out here, and she's not able to care for herself, let alone your mother. She really needs to go home."

Zahera looked from her mother to her sister. Neha was talking with some of the neighbors now, rocking back and forth on her knees and laughing incongruously as she told them in quick bursts, "I've seen the black *baba*, the black *baba*. He said I'm not in this world for much longer! Ha!"

"Yes! *You* come and stay with me!" Zahera's mother pleaded in a desperate voice, turning toward her daughter. "There's no one else!"

"They should *both* come home," I said to Zahera again.

We talked about the logistics of getting everyone back to the city. Zahera nodded her head, but she seemed uncommitted.

"Do you want to go see the *mazar*?" She asked suddenly. "Come, I'll show you!"

I agreed, as I knew she was eager for a distraction— eager to make this into a lighthearted sightseeing trip instead of a sobering window into her tragic family life. If she didn't grab onto the opportunities to make good memories right then, in the midst of crisis, then she would never have any good memories. In Zahera's world, crisis was a permanent state of being.

She led us around the side of the veranda and up a flight of steps onto a raised marble courtyard with a brightly colored shrine in the middle: a white and green mosque in miniature, complete with soaring minarets and Arabic script carved into archways over the doors. A small crowd of devotees sat or reclined under a tin roof in front of the main entrance. Some were praying aloud, others cried out in anguished wails. One woman rocked back and forth and pressed her head against the wall, beating her hands on the hard plaster again and again as she sobbed, "*Baba*, release me! Release me!"

Neha was circling the shrine in a hurried, unsteady gait, babbling to herself and staring wildly with a feverish look in her eyes. Andy and I were both deeply disturbed by the scene, but Zahera seemed undaunted.

"Isn't it beautiful?" she asked, looking admiringly at the shrine. "Let's walk around so you can see the other side."

As we made our circuit around the shrine, we passed a young woman who was kneeling on the ground with her hands knotted behind her back as if they were tied together. Suddenly she shrieked and began to flail and throw her body against the marble. We stood watching her for a moment, unsure if she was in the throes of demonic possession or a psychotic episode—and with no idea what to do. Zahera seemed uncomfortable as well, but perhaps from our dismay rather than from the sight of the girl. She had spent many months living at that *mazar*, and the broken bodies and mental illness would have been nothing new to her.

She quickly led us to the opposite side of the courtyard, where a low railing overlooked an open expanse of water and tropical foliage. It was beautiful, but as the backdrop for this strange place so full of suffering and insanity, the empty, borderless swamp only added to my sense of desolation. We seemed to be standing on a forgotten corner at the very edges of the earth. Andy took a photo of us in front of the watery, green landscape.

When we returned to the family's small enclosure on the veranda, Zahera told us matter-of-factly that Neha couldn't go home with us that day.

"She won't be able to cook, and she doesn't know how to keep house. That will make our brother angry, and he will beat her. But my grandmother is coming to visit tomorrow, so Neha can go home with her to stay in the village for a while."

"So when will you and your mother come home?" I asked.

She was silent for a moment, her face serious. Then she said, "My mother has taken a vow to stay here at the *mazar* until Moharram, and she won't be willing to leave before that. So I'll just have to stay here with her until then."

"But that's another three months away!" I protested.

She shrugged, and her face betrayed no emotion. "*Ham kyaa kare?*" (What can I do?) Without a second thought, she had decided to remain in that isolated village for the next three months, suffering the heat and the mosquitoes so that she could care for her mentally ill mother.

When it was time to leave, I broke down crying.

"So. Now there won't be a chance for us to meet again, before you go back to your country?" Zahera asked, smiling sadly. She hugged me and said, "Don't cry!" as she wiped away my tears.

As we turned to go, Neha smiled brightly and waved goodbye from the veranda. I was struck by the transparency and honesty of her face, and I thought back to what Amna had once told me: "Everyone thinks that girl is stupid. She's not stupid! She's just honest. She's totally innocent and good."

Zahera accompanied us back through the village to the main road. I tried to savor our last few moments together and to memorize the stillness of the air, the picturesque water buffalo grazing in the fields, the familiar closeness between us. As we flagged down a taxi, my tears came again. Then Zahera and I hugged each other tightly and *salaam*'d.

"I love you!" I told her in English, because I was not used to saying it in Hindi. I had never once heard any of our neighbors use the phrase.

Zahera giggled and kissed me on the cheek, replying in sing-song English, "I love you, too!"

Andy and I opened the back hatch of the jeep taxi and sat down, facing Zahera as the taxi pulled away from her. She was blurry through my tears, growing smaller and smaller as she stood on the side of the road in that tiny outpost, waving and smiling, with no one to look after her, and so many responsibilities on her young shoulders. I was awed by her courage and even joy in the midst of such terrible circumstances, circumstances that I knew would continue long after we were gone. *Ham kyaa kare?* What could I do?

13
LEAVING HOME

September 6, 2014

"If you came back, you wanted to leave again; if you went away, you longed to come back. Wherever you were, you could hear the call of the homeland, like the note of a herdsman's horn far away in the hills. You had one home out there, and one home over here, and yet you were an alien in both places. Your true abiding place was the vision of something very far off, and your soul was like the waves, always restless, forever in motion."

—from *The Emigrants* by John Bojer

At eight o'clock in the morning on our last day, my neighbor Hina came over to see me. When she found out I was bathing, she simply waited outside until I was finished, talking to me through the curtain intermittently until I emerged from the "bathroom" and went inside. Then she stood over Andy and me as we sat down to eat our breakfast. Finally, I told her directly that we needed to eat, but we would come by to visit her family in the afternoon. Reluctantly, she retreated down the stairs.

"This is going to be a long day," I said.

After we carried our steel trunk to a neighbor's house that afternoon, the free-for-all began. Because we were giving away all of our things, and because our neighbors had learned over the course of their lives that worth and love were demonstrated through material gifts, we knew that many people would be eager to lay claim to whatever they could. Who wouldn't want to cut down the time they spent cooking over a hot, smoky fire by replacing their primitive pot with a pressure cooker? Or exchange their sagging, broken *taakat* with a newer one whose wooden slats were still parallel to each other? There were plenty of odds and ends that hadn't been promised to anyone in advance, but I grew stressed as I tried to compute how many things there were and who they should be given to.

Our *taakat* was by far the most valuable item. We had decided to give it to Meena, the woman who was perhaps the poorest individual in our community, assuming that most people wouldn't push too hard for possession of the bed when they found out it was going to a disabled widow with three young girls.

But people did argue. The woman whose roof practically joined with ours and whose stairwell we needed to use in order to get the bed down from our room said, "You're going to have to bring the *taakat* through my house anyway. You might as well just leave it there."

The most stressful point of the day came after we called a few specific people to our house to pick up the particular items we had promised in advance. When others in the community realized what was going on, they followed along uninvited, which resulted in a mob inside our small room as everyone shouted, pleaded, wheedled, and demanded knick-knacks, kitchen implements, and furniture.

The neighbor who had demanded the *taakat* tried to wrench a large pot out of my arms after I refused to give it to her. My eyes widened in disbelief. "Are you going to just TAKE things by force? Really?"

The question seemed to bring the crowd to their senses and many people quieted down. Even my neighbor seemed slightly ashamed of her behavior.

But soon the clamor of claims and counter-claims rose back to full volume. With the crowd closing in around me, I hugged the stack of remaining dishes and kitchenware against my chest, struggling to make a decision about how to get rid of them.

Unable to piece together a single thought as the demanding crowd engulfed me, I finally broke down crying. "Everyone needs to leave. Please go away. I can't think clearly, and I just need to be alone for a little while."

Several people said to one another, "Look! Umera is so worried that she's crying. We've really made her distressed." But no one left. Everyone remained standing where they were.

I raised my voice. "I need everyone to leave! Go outside!"

Andy helped herd people out of the door, gently pushing some and finally pressing the door closed against those who were most reluctant to leave. One of the men from our alleyway made himself the unofficial bouncer, angrily shooing away others with great gusto, but never stepping through the doorway himself. He was surprised when Andy asked him to leave as well.

After firmly bolting the door, I sat down on the floor to collect myself, still hearing the lively chatter of the masses just outside my door. What had happened was one step short of looting, and I was hurt by our neighbors' insensitive, selfish behavior. *After all this time, does it really just come down to stuff?* I wondered. *Are we still just "walking wallets," charitable patrons instead of friends?*

Just then, three of my friends appeared in the stairwell. "We don't want anything," they said through the closed door. "We just came out of love. To see you."

I ushered them into the room, forcefully shutting the door against those who were still trying to come inside. After locking the door, I turned to face my friends. "I'm glad you came."

"Have you made dinner?" one of them asked.

"We'll eat at Amna's house tonight—they've invited us," I said.

"Okay," she said, "because if you didn't have plans, I was going to invite you and Andy to eat at my house tonight."

The kindness of her invitation overwhelmed me, and I hugged her, on the verge of tears. She was the first person all afternoon to express concern for my welfare and to anticipate my needs instead of only thinking about what she could get out of me before I left.

By late afternoon, Andy and I had finished making our final visits to friends' houses and were making last-minute preparations before heading to Amna's house to eat. Plenty of people were still hanging around, but most of them had the good sense at this point not to ask for anything else—most, but not all. An auntie from down the street made one last exasperating attempt to cajole us into changing our minds about giving her the bamboo shelves we had already promised to someone else. Andy's repeated attempts to explain our logic seemed to be going nowhere.

Eventually, she raised an aggressive finger in front of him. "Wait a minute. Are you saying that the people who ask for things *won't* get them, and the people who don't ask for things *will*?!" Her angry eyebrows were knit together in incredulity.

Now Andy couldn't help laughing. "That's exactly what I am saying," he said with a good-natured grin. The rest of the crowd chuckled as they repeated the amusing riddle to one another.

Just then, another neighbor appeared in the doorway, smiling shyly. "I brought a gift for you," she said, holding out a little box wrapped in shiny red paper.

I felt my soul being mended a little further, restoring my sense of love and belonging in the community, replacing the disappointment and hurt I had felt earlier.

As soon as I walked into Amna's house, I immediately began unloading my stress and sadness over the way people had behaved during the afternoon. The family was sympathetic and disapproving of the way people had seemed to care more about getting our stuff than they did about saying goodbye.

Using the acrylic paints and watercolor paper I had given her a few days before, Amna's daughter Shabana had created a painting for Andy and me to take with us— three roses, one budding, one half-opened, and one in full bloom, against a vibrant green background with a butterfly hovering in the corner.

After she presented us with our gift, the eight of us sat in a circle on the family's *taakat* and ate generous helpings of fragrant chicken biryani in silence, savoring the flavors of cardamom and a last meal together.

"I'm very sad," Amna kept saying, barely keeping tears at bay. Most people used the Muslim custom of three quick embraces on alternating sides, but when we stood to leave, she hugged me for a long time, holding me tightly like my mother had done when I had left America to come to India. I kissed her on the cheek, thinking of how she had become a mother figure for me in many ways.

When we walked back to our room after dinner to get our luggage, we found a small crowd standing in the alley outside our door.

"We're all waiting for you!" they said. "We're going to send you off."

They followed us up the stairs and into our room, which became more and more crowded as others streamed in to catch the last few moments with us while we double-checked that nothing had been left behind. We were all joking around, everyone laughing and smiling, but they watched us intently.

I picked up Firoz, the toddler who lived downstairs, to hug and kiss him goodbye. I patted his chubby belly one last time and set him back down on the floor, feeling like I might cry. I wanted to hug his mother—our landlady—too, but she seemed distant and stiff when I touched her shoulder to say goodbye.

Then it was time to go. We strapped on our giant back-packs. As we stepped out the door, I realized that Firoz's mother wasn't with us. I stepped back inside the house to ask about her, and the others in the house started calling her name. She came down the stairs slowly, her face closed, her brow furrowed. She reached the bottom of the stairs, and as I reached out to embrace her, she broke down sobbing, unable to look up or speak.

"Come on, come out with us to the road," I said, taking her hand. But she broke away and retreated into her room. Two days later, she would call me while we were in Delhi, just hours away from boarding the plane, and hearing my voice over the phone she would break down crying again. Then she would take a few moments to collect herself while quickly putting Firoz on the phone, coaching him to say, "*Bhabi, vaapas aao*—Sister-in-law, come back."

Surrounded by the tearful smiles of our friends and neighbors, we turned the corner onto the alleyway leading to the main road just as the *azaan* began. I was reminded of all the funeral processions we had seen, bodies being carried out to the graveyard as the call to prayer sounded overhead. As the large crowd of people—men and women, some crying, some somber—escorted us out of the community for the last time, this, too, felt like a funeral procession.

At the edge of the slum, the profusion of people spilled out into the road, stopping traffic while everyone hugged us and said goodbye—*"A-salaam-walei-kum," "Allah hafiz," "Khuda hafiz." Peace be with you. May God be your Guardian.* As our landlord's elderly mother hugged me, she surprised me with her tears.

A smaller group crossed the road with us and helped to flag down an auto. There was one last round of goodbyes while we packed our luggage into the back and sat inside. I could see Firoz's little face in the panorama of waving people as we pulled away. He looked confused and worried as he stared at us.

Throughout the day, I had felt waves of sadness, anger, tenderness, frustration, laughter, happiness, and grief—experiencing in one day the full range of emotions I had felt throughout our time in India. I felt exhausted by everyone's desire to be with us as much as possible in those last hours. I felt overwhelmed by the intensity of their need. I was humbled by and grateful for the many gifts we had received.

"Just think," our former landlady Gita had told us earlier that week, "when you first arrived here, no one even wanted to offer you a room, because they didn't know you. Now there's not a single person in this neighborhood who isn't sad you're leaving."

Her words expressed the heart and soul of our time in India. I would feel many things about leaving over the coming months, but in that moment, the only thing I felt was immeasurable loss.

VI.
HEALING

September 2014—July 2015

"Out beyond ideas of wrongdoing and rightdoing,
there is a field. I'll meet you there.

When the soul lies down in that grass,
the world is too full to talk about."

–Jalahuddin Rumi

14
PARADOX

"Find the real world, give it endlessly away, grow rich flinging gold to all who ask. Live at the empty heart of paradox. I'll dance with you there—cheek to cheek."

—Rumi

After nearly four years abroad, Andy and I had no home to return to. We had never lived in the West as a married couple, and neither of us felt any connection to the town where I had grown up or to the city where Andy had attended high school. Returning to the American South or the conservative, evangelical context we had grown up in was not an appealing option. Our families and friends were scattered across the continent, and we felt that even if we chose to settle near a few of them, it would be impossible to slip into "normal life" in a context where few people were able to understand or relate to our experiences, and where our community would likely expect us to think and behave like the people we had been when we moved to India—people we no longer were.

India had become our home, and it was no longer possible for us to live there, so in a sense we felt like refugees—exiles for whom home no longer exists. We had been stripped of any familiar geography, community, or culture, and our interior landscape had shifted as well. Gone were the theological language, the spiritual certainty, and the identities that had formed the support beams of our lives before we had moved to India. That house was no longer standing, and we were not yet sure what was taking shape in its place.

Given our sense of vulnerability and dislocation, we felt it was important to be supported by our broader Servants family as we transitioned back into life in North America. So upon leaving India, we moved to Vancouver, British Columbia, to live in a Servants' community house in the impoverished area of the city, known locally as the Downtown Eastside.

***

On our first Sunday in Vancouver, I found myself sitting, somewhat reluctantly, in a church pew. Other people in our house attended most weeks, and this church in particular had a long history with Servants, having financially supported a handful of other long-term workers in poor, urban communities in Asia. So because we had nothing else planned for the day—and because we thought we should make an effort to begin making friends in this new city—we decided to go to church with our housemates.

Our expectations were low. We had never found a church home while in India, and we had grown so used to being lonely voices on the outskirts of the Christian world that we had begun to lose hope that we would ever find a place of belonging within it. The churches we had encountered in India had seemed so disconnected from the struggle for justice and the plight of the poor. And over time, as our experiences had continued to raise new doubts and questions, we had increasingly felt the need to filter what we shared with friends and church connections back in the United States, because many of them were uncomfortable with both our emphasis on justice and our increasing theological uncertainty. One church had even stopped financially supporting us after they found out that we did not believe our neighbors were bound for hell unless they converted to Christianity. Since we were spending time building friendships and working to improve our neighbors' lives, but were not seeking to convert them, the pastor explained that there was not enough money in the church's budget for a ministry as "unfocused" as ours. As one of the church staff members remarked, "We understand that you need to focus on stuff like clean water in your context, because people are poor. But people in our congregation already have their basic needs met, so we need to focus on something else."

So on that Sunday morning, just a few days after arriving in Vancouver, I was surprised to encounter Jesus in one of the last places I expected to find Him: during the worship service at the church we attended with our housemates. Light spilled through stained-glass windows onto a gaggle of unruly children who sat on the steps in front of the altar. The pastor asked them questions, engaged with their meandering responses, and then led them in a simple prayer. They played with the careless abandon of children who feel safe, surrounded by a community of patient and loving adults.

Seeing the delight that the entire congregation took in including small children in the service gave me hope. So did the fact that there was a grey-haired woman who felt free to dance in the aisle while the rest of us sang worship songs with typical Baptist understatement, slightly swaying or clapping where we stood. After seeing so much ugliness in the world, I needed to see people loving each other well. I needed to see little people and weak people and strange people valued and welcomed as individuals who have important contributions to make. That is what I saw during this service, and I drank it in like medicine.

One of the pastors introduced himself after the service and unleashed a flood of sadness in me with a simple question about where we had come from. Everything was so raw that I couldn't imagine answering his question in ten thousand words or less, and instead I broke down sobbing.

In fact, I sobbed during church every week for a while. I couldn't go through the communion line to receive the Body and Blood of Jesus without crying, and I wondered if other people thought I was crazy and unstable. Feeling entirely unmoored, I wondered if I was.

I could not rationally explain to anyone what it was that moved me so deeply. I felt drawn to the beauty and love of God in that place through those people. My soul ached with the intensity of my longing and with the relief of finally being nourished by the Living Bread for which I had been so desperately hungry.

I was awed by Jesus' humility as He offered Himself to me every week—even those weeks when I was not sure if I was a Christian anymore, or if I wanted to be. Even the weeks I thought I didn't have it in me to inconvenience, much less sacrifice, myself for anyone ever again.

I felt like a failure, like the Apostle Peter—except I wasn't so sure that, like Peter, I would be able to overcome my fears and decide to keep following Jesus anyway, now that I knew what crucifixion really meant. I was overwhelmed by what I felt each time I made my way down the aisle to stand in front of Jesus and look Him in the eye. But every Sunday, the invitation continued to be pressed into my hands.

"This is the Body of Christ, broken for you," Christ would say through the woman or man who handed me the bread. *This is the love that is big enough to hold you even though you are calloused and afraid. This is the community that you are invited to continue loving and being loved by.*

As I embarked on the journey toward deeper healing, this love and this community held me, a cast wrapped around these broken bones.

***

As we joined the Servants community in their rhythms of prayer, shared life, and hospitality, the friendships we developed with our housemates provided the support we needed during this vulnerable time, and we appreciated the continuity of belonging to the Servants community even though we had left our team, our neighborhood, and almost every other aspect of our old lives behind. Certain aspects of that continuity were not entirely helpful, however, since many of the most stressful elements of our life in India carried over into life in Vancouver. For although we were no longer in an Asian slum, we had immersed ourselves in a new context of Western poverty—one characterized by mental illness and addiction, in addition to structural injustices. The community we had joined was committed to journeying alongside people whose lives, like those of our Indian neighbors, were shaped by poverty and trauma.

My flimsy mental and emotional boundaries continued to be strained by the stresses of shared space, needy neighbors, and unpredictability. Every time the doorbell or the phone rang at the community house, I experienced the same anxiety-induced paralysis that had plagued me in the slum: I was unable to answer the door or the phone, and I was unable to cope with the constant, unsettling feeling that my space and time could be invaded at any moment. Being with people exhausted me, and the idea of being "trapped" in social interactions and obligations over which I had no control caused me to shut down emotionally.

I was bewildered by my brittle emotional condition and by my utter lack of flexibility or tolerance for uncertainty. I felt guilty about my inability—and my complete lack of interest—in forging friendships with my new neighbors. Andy was often as flummoxed by my behavior as I was— even though I was struggling with community life, he seemed to adjust quickly to the contours of our new situation. I once sat upstairs in our bedroom, listening to a raucous community dinner and Christmas party going on beneath the floorboards, for hours without being able to summon the courage to go downstairs and join in—though I was supposed to be one of the hosts. I could not will myself to feel or to be otherwise. I was still reeling from India; gasping for air. I wondered whether this was all temporary, or whether I was a rubber band that had been stretched so far that it had snapped.

In early December, my desperation drove me to attempt something I never would have considered before: a silent retreat. As an extrovert, I had always thrived on connection with other people. For me, the idea of giving up communication and verbal expression was akin to dying, so I approached the three days of silence with trepidation—yet at the same time, I felt mysteriously drawn toward silence and that inexplicable pull motivated me to push through my anxiety in the face of the unknown. It was as though God Herself was inviting me, but I knew not where. During that retreat, I began to come to terms with myself—accepting the full range of my emotions, desires, problems, and life history without fearing or rejecting anything. The entire time, there was a song stuck in my head. The voice looping in my mind was that of twenty-first century English singer-songwriter Nick Mulvey, but the lyrics were based on a poem by thirteenth-century Sufi mystic Jalahuddin Rumi:

Out beyond ideas of wrongdoing and rightdoing, there is a field. I'll meet you there.

A few weeks after my silent retreat, Andy and I both began to feel that we needed to move out of the Servants house and live on our own. Andy was not feeling as worn down by India or as emotionally fragile as I was, but he was concerned that I was continuing to struggle emotionally. He also felt drawn toward full-time employment and further study, commitments which would have been impossible to juggle with the intensive demands of community living.

Although it was becoming increasingly clear that we were ill-equipped to handle the intensity of life in the Servants community, we struggled with guilt about abandoning life with people in poverty again. But then we remembered those whispers of freedom we had sensed when we were in Darjeeling, and we found the courage to let go of the last straw of our self-made identity. Up to that point, we had held onto it for safekeeping, just in case: *we still live with the poor!* Yet we now knew that the uncharted season we were moving into would require more than leaving India behind. True rest would require laying aside intensive relational involvement with the poor for a time as well.

After Andy and I decided that we were going to leave the Servants community, I felt giddy as I imagined the freedom and privacy we would enjoy in an apartment of our own. At the same time, I was distressed by my need for solitude and predictability, and I sometimes wondered if my heightened desire for time and space alone meant that I was slipping dangerously toward isolation and away from solidarity.

***

Near the end of our time with Servants, our friend Jo, the staff person responsible for member care, facilitated a debriefing retreat for Andy and me at a cozy lodge nestled in the evergreen hills of a small island off the coast of British Columbia. During that time, we remembered and processed our lives in India. Sharing our individual accounts of significant events with one another helped Andy and me to understand the unique ways that each of us had interpreted and been impacted by the same experiences.

Andy felt more sadness than I did at the time. I was numb to my grief, and when I thought about the slum, I mostly felt stress, anger, and relief that we were no longer in India. I almost felt as though I had to hold onto those negative feelings to the exclusion of all else in order to justify my departure—to myself as much as to anyone else. But Jo encouraged me to reflect on the idea of paradox. "You can both love India and hate India at the same time," she explained. "You don't have to choose."

In the months leading up to our retreat, I had vacillated between two conflicting perspectives on the chapter of my life that I had spent in India. When I was in a better emotional space—feeling more grounded, more connected to God—I would think, "India was a necessary part of my spiritual journey. God led me there, taught me so much, gave me beautiful friendships, guided me through unique and meaningful experiences, and She has brought good out of everything." When I considered how my life in the slum had caused me to grow in my experience of God, my connection to the world, and my knowledge of myself, I felt incredibly thankful for the journey. I would remind myself that my time in the slums had brought me to the place I needed to be in order to heal from the wounds that I carried with me to India.

But when I grew frustrated and discouraged—which was most of the time—I would revert to dark thoughts about how India had messed up my life. I would tell myself that it had been a mistake to move there in the first place. I would reflect bitterly about how "behind" I was in life because I had no work history, no professional credentials, no close friends or connection to any place in particular. I felt frustrated by the way that the immigration process to Canada put my life on hold, and I felt angry that I had no home to go back to in the States or anywhere else. When these despairing thoughts took over, I felt disappointed with myself, because we had nothing to show for all our effort over the past few years.

I had spent so much time ricocheting between these two extremes as I struggled in vain to decide which version was accurate. By the time we were debriefing with Jo, I was leaning toward believing the second narrative to the exclusion of the first. I felt bitter rather than thankful. Jo's suggestion that I accept the confusing, parallel existence of these two perspectives lifted a huge weight off my mind, liberating me to feel both joy and regret about our time in India. My longing for India and my hatred of India could coexist.

For the first time in several months, I was able to access tender, positive emotions toward the places and people that had made up my life in Ilahabad: the delight in watching two-year-old Firoz joyfully throw dippers of water over his head, missing his soapy hair entirely, in an adorable attempt to bathe himself while his mother and I filled our water drum from a hose every morning. The warmth in the smiles of the aunties who would affectionately pat the space next to them on the *taakat,* inviting me to join their conversation as they sat together, sorting weevils out of the rice for the evening meal.

At the lodge, I spent an entire day creating a timeline of the years I had spent in the slums, mapping out the events and people who had shaped our lives and changed us. Then I spent an hour sharing that timeline with Jo, exploring moments of joy and loss, of hope and disappointment. Jo didn't know anything about the retreat I had taken back in December, but when she began praying for me after I shared my story, she began quoting the same poem of Rumi's which had become the theme of those three silent, soul-searching days: "Out beyond ideas of wrongdoing and rightdoing, there is a field. I'll meet you there." She then went on to quote another verse of Rumi's, one which perfectly summed up the theme of embracing paradox which had characterized my last few days at the lodge: "Live at the empty heart of paradox. I'll dance with you there—cheek to cheek."

Her words filled me with hope. After all that had happened—the ceaseless suffering and unresolved questions and unfinished dreams—I had begun to wonder if there was any real journey or destination in life, or if we were all simply striving to make meaning out of our arbitrary wandering through a disconnected series of events. In the haze of depression, I had begun to question whether God was just an impersonal energy of love flowing through the world—beautiful, important, and very real, but not an entity that could be known personally, relationally, intimately.

Yet God seemed to speak to me through Jo's words, conveying Her presence with me on this journey. Our debriefing retreat was connected to my silent retreat. This day was connected to every day that had come before it. God did not exist in the same way as gravity or molecular structure, but was a personal presence who was guiding me—or at least traveling beside me—along this path.

That night, for the first time in a long while, I began to pray. I sat in a quiet room alone, giving myself over to the silence. I felt a warm stillness inside of me, a sense of love and contentment that washed over me like a slow-breaking wave. I thought of my neighbors, and I felt a sense of immediacy and connection—as if I were in the slum with them again.

To my surprise, I also experienced the transcendent feeling that even as I had "traveled" back to them, I remained in the peaceful, loving presence of God: the slum and everyone who lived there was bathed in it. I was in the presence of God and my neighbors at the same time—or, more accurately, I was in God and interacting with my neighbors *through* or *from within* God. Standing with Zahera, with Amna and her family, with Meena and her daughters, and with everyone else, I felt no anxiety or resentment or stress. Neither did I feel the crushing sadness that I had so often experienced in their midst. I felt only love, peace, and light, and I prayed those things over them. A Hindi song rose within me, and I began to sing, over and over, my prayer for the beloved community I had left behind:

Shanti, shanti, shanti ho,
Charon teraf teri shanti ho.

Peace, peace, peace be,
On all four sides, Your peace be.

This sense of peace settled into my heart and remained. Though I still had no idea what lay ahead of me, the uncertainty didn't bother me anymore.

That night, Jo asked us to write down some of the experiences we treasured about our time in India and some that had been difficult. We gathered around a fireplace in the main room of the lodge and kindled a fire. "When you're ready," Jo said, "place these experiences into the fire and release them to God."

I took a deep breath, crumpled my paper into a ball and tossed it into the flames. The fire licked at the edges of the paper, and then engulfed my joys and sorrows in a crackling blaze. As I watched the embers turn to ash, the hard shell of bitterness around my heart burned away, and I felt the extent of my loss for the first time since leaving India. The tears came at last, and I wept in remembrance and gratitude for all that had been.

15
WOMB TIME

"I believe that Christ came not to dispel the darkness but to teach us to dwell with integrity, compassion, and love in the midst of ambiguity. The one who grew in the fertile darkness of Mary's womb knew that darkness is not evil of itself. Rather, it can become the tending place in which our longings for healing, justice and peace grow and come to birth."

—Jan L. Richardson

Despite these moments of consolation and healing, I continued to battle with feelings of discouragement and regret throughout my first year in Canada. I often felt useless, trapped, and hopeless as I struggled to find a meaningful way to use my time. As an American, I was unable to work until I could secure official status in Canada, and the waiting period for my permanent residency application prevented me from following my impulse to quickly find some new role or work with which to define myself. I was frustrated by the feeling that I was wasting time sitting idle. When Andy began working a full-time job, which came more swiftly since his citizenship gave him the right to work in Canada, my days were long and lonely. I felt isolated, and I struggled with the sense that my life had gone off track in a way that I would never be able to correct. At twenty-six, I had no job, no established friendships, no clear plan for the future, and I felt like a husk of my former self.

My spiritual director sometimes reminds me that spiritual growth is not a linear process. It is more of a spiral, she says, so that each time we return to the same issue, we address it at a deeper level. It is God's mercy that She allows us to chip away at things gradually rather than forcing us to confront ourselves all at once and become overwhelmed. That downward spiral certainly describes my own journey. As I spoke with my spiritual director about my sense of entrapment, of being walled in on all sides, she repeated the word "trapped" back to me thoughtfully. "How do you think God sees it?" she asked.

In the silence that followed, an image of a broken arm in a sling came to mind. After all the fury I had expressed about my arbitrary "punishment," I was almost too embarrassed to vocalize what I had seen. Suddenly it was clear that I was not trapped in a prison, as I had supposed; instead, I was being held still for long enough to heal. The uncomfortable constraints were protective, not oppressive, and they would be removed as soon as I was well enough to carry on without them. As I reflected on this image, I knew that what I really needed was not a busy schedule to take the edge off the pain of my deeper yearnings and questions. What I needed—and what I was getting—was the chance to detox from busyness and from centering my life and identity around helping others.

***

Later that spring, I dreamt that I was pregnant. My belly was full and round, and I felt my body beginning the painful contractions of labor. I rushed to the hospital to give birth, but after examining me, the doctors informed me that I was nowhere near ready.

"What?" I asked in amazement. "What do you mean I'm not in labor?"

They laughed. "Go home. We'll see you in six months."

I woke with sadness because I knew with painful certainty exactly what the dream meant: here I was thinking that this excruciating season of rest and preparation was over, and I was ready to leap into the next phase. The extreme discomfort of the liminal space I was occupying made me feel sure that it had reached its fullness, but in reality there was more to come: something new was growing inside me, but God had not yet birthed it. *Be patient*, the dream advised.

These images—of a healing wound and pregnancy—did not change my overall experience of the dark months of uncertainty, when anxiety sometimes gave way to depression, and it was difficult for me to imagine the way forward. But in moments of stillness—the brief times when I was able to release my grasp on future plans and relax into openness and receptivity—these images were reassuring signposts on the journey. They reminded me that I am not alone, that all is not arbitrary chaos. Storms may continue at the surface, but deep within there is a new calm rising. God keeps reaching out to reassure me that all is not lost, and I am holding onto those whispers of hope like a lifeline.

Epilogue

"Leaving home is living as though I do not yet have a home, and must look far and wide to find one. Home is the center of my being, where I can hear the voice that says, "You are my beloved. On you my favor rests"... The same voice that speaks to all the children of God and sets them free to live in the midst of a dark world while remaining in the light."

—Henri Nouwen

Though I no longer live in the slum, I have not returned to the life I knew in the West before I met Amna, Zahera, Meena, and the many other friends whose stories merged with mine. Though I have been stripped and pruned of my certainty and plans, I am growing back like a spring vine. Though I bear the mark of the suffering I have witnessed, I also bear signs of new life.

As I write, I am sitting at a quiet desk in my well-ventilated, third-floor attic suite in Vancouver, one of the most livable cities in the world. I no longer need to rely on a fan to keep the noise and heat rash at bay, as I did in our Indian slum. I look out at the leafy green trees of our quiet, middle-class neighborhood, and memories of our time in India press against me and push me toward new questions as I seek to integrate our season there with my life before India and the life I am tending now in Canada.

Looking back, I can trace the naiveté and youthful idealism that carried us to India. We went partly out of principle, partly out of a desire to prove ourselves by doing something very difficult, and partly to have an adventure—though at the time, these latter two motivations operated somewhat outside of our conscious awareness. We thought that wanting to be hardcore was a virtue in itself, because it signaled total commitment, so we didn't analyze the role of our egos in propelling us toward extremes.

As I reflect on our time there, I could tell you about the ways that living in the slums has solidified our commitment to simple living and continues to influence all sorts of choices in our day-to-day lives. I could also tell you how seeing things through our neighbors' eyes in India has changed our own perspective on nearly everything, how befriending village migrants has sparked Andy's interest in learning how to farm, or how the experience of living as a foreigner in another country has continued to draw me into friendships with undocumented immigrants and refugees here in Vancouver.

But the deeper and more significant changes are more difficult to explain. External measurements and rules and lifestyle choices no longer define whether I am living faithfully in the world. I am no longer inclined to define myself in terms of what I do or how I live. To be honest, I feel more uncertain about the future than I ever have before.

I am struggling to maintain a healthy detachment, or a "spiritual indifference," that will free me to apply the full force of my efforts passionately toward something without the expectation that my faithful actions will also prove effective in the end. Because I am immersed in a culture that values achievement, productivity, and instant gratification, I must resist the temptation to try to change the world, even as I refuse to despair about our limited ability to bring about change over the long haul.

Slowly, I am learning to set healthy boundaries around my time, energy, and emotional capacity, because I have come to see how knowing these limits can be a gift to the people around me. Slowly, I am learning to make my home in God. After I take time to rest in Her presence, to connect with myself and reflect on my attitudes and motivations, and to ground myself in my identity apart from what I do for others or how they perceive me, I am able to offer my presence to others in a deeper and more authentic way than if I am preoccupied with anxiety, resentment, or stress. I have realized that tending to Jesus in other people and recognizing Him in myself are part of the same thing, and that my capacity for loving others is dependent on my capacity to love myself.

As we learn what it means to care for ourselves, Andy and I are currently living closer to "isolation" than we are to "solidarity." Our lives have boomeranged all over this continuum, and we will *always* be figuring this out, fine-tuning at some times and making quantum leaps at others. We've accepted that life comes in seasons and that listening to the untamed Spirit of God is more important than grading ourselves against a rubric. Future seasons may well challenge me to grow into community and reorganize my life yet again. But for now, I am simply trying to be faithful to the practical actions and heart attitudes that underpin community life: interdependence, hospitality, love, and sacrifice. Community is not ultimately about outward forms, but about a willingness to engage deeply with others and to be changed by them, as painful or humbling as it may be.

Though my idealism has floundered, I am learning the gritty essence of hope. Though many days I don't know what I believe, I know more clearly the God I aspire to believe in. As my childhood shadow-version of an angry, small god recedes, I am becoming more certain of God's love for me—for all of us—than I have ever been in my life. For even and especially in the midst of my closed-fisted stubbornness, laziness, fear, and despair, I am learning to experience God's unconditional love as an unearned grace.

ACKNOWLEDGMENTS

First, I would like to thank my husband, Andy, for living with me the journey that is recorded in these pages, and for patiently supporting me—both through the darkest days post-India, and through the process of writing this book. You are the most amazing friend, lover, life partner, and co-adventurer I could ever ask for.

This book would not be what it is without my incredibly gifted editor-cum-spiritual director, Karen Hollenbeck Wuest, who saw glimmers of the deeper story in the earliest version of my manuscript, and companioned me through the difficult process of excavating my inner journey beneath the chaos of external events in India. For all your wisdom and guidance, I am deeply grateful.

Thanks to Caleb Ng and Jacqueline Dewar for reading and providing valuable feedback on the earliest kernels of this book. Drew Lewis, Craig Greenfield, Gerry Schoberg, Marnie Wooding, Scott Bessenecker and Tim Dickau read an extremely long early draft of the manuscript, encouraging me to continue the project, and offering professional advice on the publishing world. I would also like to thank Andrea Armstrong for creating a beautiful cover design that visually captures the form and feel of this book, and Lucas Lee for proofreading the manuscript and offering his valuable, outside perspective.

I am grateful to our Servants teammates in India, with whom we shared this formative season of our lives, for their friendship and support. I have learned so much from you, and you continue to inspire me with your faithfulness, wisdom, and love.

Thank you to the Servants team in Vancouver, who welcomed Andy and me into their community at a time when I was fragile and unable to offer anything in return for their hospitality. Through you, I experienced the welcome of Christ.

I am also grateful to the friends, family, and supporters who followed our journey in India, offered a listening ear, generously hosted Andy and me whenever we visited the U.S. You made our presence in the slum possible through your financial support, your friendship, and your prayerful encouragement.

Finally, I owe deep gratitude to my friends and neighbors in India who welcomed Andy and me into their community as strangers and made us their family. *Hamare parivar, hamare dost*: you shared your lives and your stories with us, and taught us so much about our God, our world, and ourselves. You have changed me irrevocably, and I will never forget you.